THE TECHNIQUES OF INSTRUCTION

This book is dedicated to my mother, Edith James – she has not had a book dedicated to her before but she deserves to have at least one!

THE
TECHNIQUES
OF
INSTRUCTION

ROGER JAMES

Gower

Published by
Gower Publishing Limited
Gower House
Croft Road
Aldershot
Hampshire GU11 3HR
England

Gower
Old Post Road
Brookfield
Vermont 05036
USA

Roger James has asserted his right under the Copyright, Designs and Patents Act 1988 to be identified as the author of this work.

British Library Cataloguing in Publication Data
James, Roger
  Techniques of Instruction
  I. Title
  371.3028
  ISBN 0–566–07550–4

Library of Congress Cataloging-in-Publication Data
James, Roger, 1951–
    The techniques of instruction/Roger James; consultant editor,
  Billie Taylor
        p.   cm.
    Includes index.
    ISBN 0–566–07550–4
    1. Employees—Training of—Handbooks, manuals, etc.   I. Title.
  HF5549.5.T7J27   1995   95–2231
  658.3'12404—dc20   CIP

Typeset in Ehrhardt by Poole Typesetting (Wessex) Ltd, Bournemouth and printed in Great Britain by Biddles, Guildford

Contents

List of figures and tables

Figures

Tables

Preface

This book is aimed at instructors everywhere. These few (relatively few, that is) pages are an attempt to summarize and distil the essence of effective instruction. My intention is to help anyone who instructs (or who wishes to instruct) to do it effectively and to understand why they are successful. This is a book about effective instructors and the techniques they use which make them effective. I hope it will give you an idea of how to improve your own instructing as well as where to look for more information about various aspects of instruction.

Why a book about instructors and instruction? Because instruction is a topic rarely dealt with in the training literature. Where there are books about instructors they tend to be heavily based on classroom-type instruction (chalk and talk) or to be based on the personal experiences and anecdotes of the author. Obviously there is room for both these approaches and they both contribute to the sum of knowledge about instructing; but there are also drawbacks, big drawbacks, to both approaches.

First, not all instructing takes place in a classroom. Classrooms are wonderful places designed for passing over knowledge to groups of trainees (or students). The instruction techniques relevant to classrooms are important tools in the trainer's toolkit. Carefully used, the classroom techniques will help the trainee's understanding to develop and grow. The drawback is that trainees usually come out of classrooms *knowing* but unable to *do*. In the absence of instruction about doing, trainees will have to teach themselves. Ideally, then, there should also be books which explain how to instruct trainees in doing, but there are very few books that explain what the instructor needs to do to help, how to do the instructing and why it works. This brings us to my second point, which is concerned with the value of personal anecdote and experience in instructing.

Many people with experience in a field of activity understandably feel that they know a lot about it. Hence they expect that we can benefit from their sharing opinion and experiences with us. Unfortunately this is not always the case. It is true that there can be a great value in sharing one's experience with others, but what works for one person in one situation does not always work for someone else in a different situation. Very often an author describing his or her experience of instruction does not explain in what circumstances the advice will work and when it won't work. You can always resort to trial and error of course, and find out by applying the advice yourself over a period of time with a range of trainees. Unfortunately there will need to be many trials and a great many errors before you begin to extract the full benefit from using the technique. That means a lot of failures for you – and, worse, for the trainees. There is an additional problem with using other people's anecdotes of 'how I did it' that you should take into account: very often, someone who is skilled at a task is not really aware of how they go about it. The result is that when they come to explain what they did they are often wrong. There are two instances of this that come from research studies and they both illustrate the point perfectly.

The first case was a study carried out at Glasgow University. Here someone invented a glass mouthpiece for a trumpet – it was constructed in such a way that high-speed (or, if you prefer, slow-motion) video recordings of the player's lips could be made. It was thus possible to observe how an expert player controlled the lips to produce complex and difficult musical effects. Interestingly, when the expert player observed the recordings of his technique he was shocked. It turned out that for many years he had been instructing his students to use their lips in a particular fashion to achieve a particular effect but did not do that himself. It was not arrogance or stupidity on his part – he genuinely believed that he used the method that he taught to others. The recording showed that he achieved the effect via a completely different method and that fact would not have been uncovered had his technique not been revealed by the high-speed video. It is no wonder his students had so much difficulty mastering that particular technique.

The second case concerns sales technique. For many years a mythology has been built up in the sales world about what actions on the part of the seller will produce a sale. Many books on sales technique are based on their authors' personal success and methods. About twenty years ago, however, a team of psychologists was asked to observe salespeople in real sales calls to see if the experts' advice was accurate. Once again, it wasn't. Either the seller did not do what he (usually it was a he being observed) thought he had done in the meeting or he did it and the sale fell through. In most cases that were observed the seller involved did not know what it was that had produced the success; hence, advice he might have given to others would have been completely incorrect. After observing many hundreds of sales calls in Europe and America the psychologists managed to identify what it was that made salespeople effective. They packaged it as a training programme and proved that it worked by watching many thousands of their trainees apply the techniques and win sales.

Using research to tell us what to do

The point about experts being unreliable sources of information on how they do what they do has also been found in other areas – industrial sewing and sport, to name but two. Who then should instructors turn to for guidance if not other, more experienced, instructors? The answer that forms the basis for this book is that they can turn to research studies of effective instruction. The two cases above show how careful research can uncover the patterns underlying a complex activity – and effective instruction is certainly complex on the surface. It is also rather simple underneath. It is the getting underneath instruction that can be difficult.

This book goes further than merely outlining techniques of instruction that personal anecdote and individual experience feel to be important. Here, I will base our discussion on research findings and the conclusions of careful studies of instruction – where they exist. It is a sad indictment of training research and training practice in this century that although instruction is the bedrock of all training very little study has been made of what makes instructors effective. It has been necessary, therefore, to cast the net wide to gather the few facts about instruction that do exist and that are also genuinely useful.

Effective instructional technique is based on two key elements: first, the instructor and what he or she must do to succeed; and second, the trainee. The trainee is so very important in training and yet most training literature forgets trainees are there. A classic case of not seeing the wood for the trees. Training is primarily about changing the behaviour of trainees – we want them to do things in the future that they cannot do now and we want them to do those things to certain standards of performance. If someone attends a training course and then cannot do what the course purports to teach them, they have not been well trained. This action basis in effective training is important. Many people think of training as the passing of facts or knowledge to the trainee, perhaps by lecture or some other classroom-based training technique. But knowing about something and being able to do it are quite different. Try teaching someone to swim by lecture and see the difference between knowing and doing on the first trip to the river.

When teaching knowledge it is important to understand how people come to *know* so that the classroom methods used are the ones that will help that process. In exactly the same way, when helping someone to *do*, it is important that the teacher understands how it is that people develop skilled action. The teacher can then choose the most useful instructional methods – the ones that will help the trainee to perform the activity to the required levels. In the industrial world effective instruction helps the trainee to develop the skill as quickly as possible, reducing training costs in the process!

This book outlines how people (trainees) come to develop skilled actions. If we know this we can then begin to think about what instructors must do to help that skill development process proceed as rapidly as possible. It uses the most recent research to build a description of the trainee's skill development process which instructors can use to help them instruct more effectively. It then turns to those rare gems of instructor research which show us what instructional techniques are most useful in helping people develop activity skills to high levels of performance as quickly as possible.

What is an instructor?

You may have noticed that the term 'instructor' has been used frequently in these first few paragraphs. But what do we mean by 'instructor'? It is important to define the term as it is used in this book because 'instructor' is a label which carries with it personal connotations. Each of us tends to have a slightly different picture of what an instructor is. For the rest of this book 'instructor' will refer to the person responsible for helping a trainee develop skilled performance at some form of activity.

It should be noted that, in this book and for the purposes of this discussion, instructor does not refer to someone standing at the front of a classroom talking to a group of trainees and attempting to pass on knowledge. Classroom lecturing is an important job and much training involves passing on knowledge. There are specific techniques for doing it effectively, and the large part of training literature dealing with instructional technique deals with classroom-based instruction of large groups of students. In this book instructor is defined differently, as someone who helps a trainee to develop and carry out skilful actions. The actions may be industrial or business skills involved in doing a job, or they may be sports-based activities. The important point is that it is actions that are being performed by the trainee and the instructor helps the process along.

It is also worth discussing the difference between an instructor, as we use the term in this book, and a coach. It will be a little confusing because the two terms are to some extent interchangeable – but only to a degree. I have defined an instructor as someone who helps a trainee to do something skilfully. In sport, the common term for this helpful person is 'coach'. In that sense the two terms are synonymous. In training, however, there is a subtle difference between the two terms. In industrial and commercial training a coach is more likely to be someone's superior who is charged with helping that person develop their already existing performance to higher levels. An instructor is more likely to be seen as someone who helps a trainee develop their ability from scratch to a given level of performance. There is therefore more separation between instruction and coaching in that environment compared to a sports environment.

In this book the industrial–commercial definitions are used for this reason: within industry, many managers are expected to coach their subordinates. This means that they must develop an already existing level of performance to a higher level of performance. Unfortunately, as with instruction, there is not much directly useful advice available on how to do it. Here, then, a coach is someone who boosts an already existing performance level and an instructor is someone who takes a trainee with no ability in a task and helps the trainee to develop that ability. Of course there is a tremendous overlap between the techniques involved in both.

Developing instructional skill

Let us now turn to one important limitation of a book acting as a vehicle for learning a practical task. In talking about the techniques of getting someone to do in a skilful manner we are, of course, using a knowledge tool – a book is organized information, it will not directly help you to do instructing. Because instructing is primarily a doing activity it really does require a good instructor to help you to instruct. This book provides practical advice on how to instruct most effectively, but by its very nature it cannot be a do-it-yourself guide – instruction is best learned via a good instructor using the sort of techniques described in this book! How will you recognize when you have a good instructor teaching you to instruct? It is simple: if you are being taught to use the techniques in this book when you instruct, and if your instructor is using the techniques described in this book to teach you, then she or he is a good instructor of instructors.

Bibliography and further reading

It seems appropriate at this point to explain why I have included bibliographies and what they mean. The descriptions in this book are based, as much as possible, on research. For some of the areas covered by the book this is probably the first time that the research sources have been assembled and so it seems worth listing them for that reason alone. But there is another reason as well: an important aspect of the book is that it provides a broad overview of the process of instruction rather than great detail. I have done that so that the main points do not become lost in a sea of detail. But because there will be many readers who want the detail I have deliberately left out, I have included bibliographies and recommended further reading where possible or appro-priate. For those readers requiring research detail I have provided primary research bibliographies. For those readers who want to be able to read more about a topic without having to wade through the complexities of research details and associated jargon I have included suggestions for further reading under a separate heading. Either or both of those groups of references should give you the additional information you want. All the articles, books and papers cited should be available from libraries, especially from libraries with access to the British Library collection.

The rest of the book

Finally, a few words about the chapters to follow. As you read through the book it will become clear that although the chapters address different aspects of instructing and the instructional process some of the material is repeated in other chapters. Why is this? It is because instruction is not something that happens on its own. An instructor needs to instruct a trainee and what the instructor does at any one time depends on what the trainee is doing at that time. The instructor and the trainee are joined together in the same way that two tango dancers weave their individual actions around their partner's actions in the course of the dance. It would be folly to try to separate the two dancers and talk about them separately, and it would be equally silly to talk about the instructor in the absence of the trainee. In just the same way as a tango is a continual pattern of movement with no joins between start and finish, the instruction process between instructor and trainee cannot be divided easily into stages without some artificiality creeping in. Inevitably, therefore, when we try to talk about the process of instruction and the techniques in the instructor's toolkit there will be some looking back at what went before and some looking forward to what will come. When we consider the learning process of the trainee we must also remember there is an instructor busily present and when we look at how the instructor uses instruction techniques we must acknowledge the trainee and the impact that instruction has on him or her. Some overlap in discussion is inevitable, even healthy, when considering such a dynamic process from different points of view. Do not let it stop you enjoying the inside story of how effective instructors develop skill in others.

Roger James

Acknowledgements

I would like to acknowledge the help and support I received from many people as I prepared this book. I could not have written it without the help of Fiona and my daughter Gwen. Both were willing to let me disappear for the long periods of time it took to write. I would also like to thank the friends and colleagues who were willing to read drafts and correct my grammar (as best they could) and tell me which parts they could not understand. If there are parts that you do not understand or sentences that are not grammatical then I am afraid that I am to blame rather than Tim Westerman, Helen Ballard or Caron Twining.

RJ

1

The role of the instructor in training

This chapter and the next are background material. Together they outline the basic process of training (as distinct from instruction) and how the instructor fits into the training process. In this chapter we will briefly examine the history of training, what it is and how it works. If you are keen to find out more about instruction and instructional techniques then you can safely skip both this chapter and the next.

Good instructors do not just make it up as they go along. Usually they are putting into practice a carefully designed training programme of some sort or another. Without the training programme the instructor will be guessing what to teach the trainee and when to teach it. Without an instructor, however, the training programme will have no effect at all. If the instructor does not instruct effectively the trainee will be unable to do what is required and the training programme, however carefully it has been designed, will have no effect. If you are to understand instructing then, you should also understand a little about training and the design of training programmes for these provide the music to which the instructor and trainee dance the instructional tango.

A brief history of training

Training is something which many people feel familiar with and yet it has a fairly recent history, particularly in industry. That is not to say that training is new or there has never been training; obviously people throughout history have learned many things and they have often had someone to teach them. However, that process has been somewhat hit-and-miss. Each teacher (be it master crafts-man, master warrior, master musician, navigator, philosopher or whatever) tended to teach in their own idiosyncratic fashion, possibly following the methods used by their own teacher. During the industrial revolution many people had to be taught how to do jobs they had never done before and training became important. The methods adopted, however, were those from an earlier era – those of master and apprentice. Young engineers were encouraged to 'stand next to Stanley' and learn by watching Stanley. In textiles young seamstresses were told to 'sit next to Nellie' until they could do the job.

Although watching another perform became a common method of learning, it was not a very efficient method of learning. At the turn of the present century the so-called scientific management methods of Taylor were intro-duced so as to make jobs more simple and one outcome of having simpler jobs was that they became easier to learn. But it was not until the Second World War that training became a serious topic of study.

Before 1939 training had been studied in an attempt to improve efficiency. Investigators in Russia, for example, attempted to discover how to train workers quickly and efficiently so that Russia could compete with the capitalist world. Unfortunately this work was not widely published in the West and even if it had been it is debatable how seriously it would have been taken, given the general attitude to Russia prevalent in the Western world in the 1930s. Meanwhile, in the USA, industrial training research was being carried out by a few people. Often this research grew out of the psychological investigation of learning. At this time (between the two world wars, that is) theorizing about learning was an important industry in its own right within academic psychology. As different schools of psychology battled it out for supremacy psychologists applied their 'pet' learning theories to industrial skills, partly to show that the learning theory they subscribed to was the only 'true' theory and partly to help industry become more competitive. The total research effort was relatively small, however, and the number of published results was also small. When the Second World War started it was a different story, however.

The military, and particularly the United States military, has always had a keen interest in training. Obviously as new weapons were developed the existing forces needed to learn how to use them as quickly as possible. Equally important, as the number of new recruits grew so did the need to train them to become effective fighting soldiers. Hence at this time an increasing number of studies of training and training methods were undertaken.

The Second World War was also significant in that much of industry changed dramatically. Many workers in industry were men and they left to become soldiers and sailors. This left a labour force vacuum rapidly filled with women encouraged into industry from their domestic roles. This influx of new workers produced a tremendous need for effective and efficient training practices. Being able to train many new workers quickly and effectively became of vital national importance, so much so that at this time research into effective industrial training became a growth area. This growth in training research continued after the war ended because the women who had been working in industry were then encouraged to return to the kitchen so that the demobbed soldiers could once again return to working in industry – creating another re-training need.

Industrial training was thus really a serious area of study only in the last fifty years or so – not long at all if you consider the importance and scope of effective training in our modern world. But the remarkable thing about the research undertaken in that time is that training instructors seem to have had very little attention paid to their role at all – at least if the amount of research into instruction is any guide! There was a good deal of investigation into whether training worked at all, investigation into discovering what were the best methods of breaking tasks down to produce training exercises, finding effective movement patterns, finding effective classroom practices, finding out how to devise programmes. But almost nothing was done to investigate instruction and the impact that instructors had on the acquisition of skill. It was almost as if instructors were beneath study – after all they were only the people who put training schemes (designed by the experts) into practice. The training scheme was the most visible sign of a company carrying out training. In all that research and writing the training scheme became more important than the instructor who put the scheme into operation.

Compared to industry the training that takes place in sport has been extensively studied, but, once again, only fairly recently. Between the wars most research took place in the USA in the competitive world of professional sport. Since the 1950s sport has become more competitive around the world and international competitions have become important sources of national prestige. Many countries have put great effort into helping their athletes to win, and an important aspect of this help is the training method used. Once again, though, the emphasis seems not to be on the instructor (or coach) but on the athlete's physiology or the training scheme used. Recent publications for different sports review training schedules for fitness, schedules for technical ability in the sport, how to motivate athletes, how to prepare athletes mentally for competition, and so on, but there is very little written about how to coach (or instruct) someone so as to help them develop their skill. As with industry, the process of instruction seems to have been largely ignored.

Instructors are a part of the training process, and without instructors training does not happen. It seems obvious to say it (but it is seldom said) but the best training programme in the world is useless without a good instructor to run it. Equally, a good instructor can turn a mediocre training programme into something rather special. However much effort is put into designing training programmes it is the instructor who turns the programme and all it contains into something from which trainees can learn. And yet, within the training world, it is the design of training and the training programme details that absorb most of the effort of professional trainers. In recognition of that we should spend a little time considering what training is about so that we can understand the place of the instructor within the larger training picture. In the next chapter we will briefly consider training to see where and how instruction and instructors fit into the training process.

Bibliography

Belbin, E., Belbin, R.M. and Hill, F. (1957), 'A Comparison between the Results of Three Different Methods of Operator Training', *Ergonomics*, 1, 39–50.

Blain, I. (1944), 'Principles of Industrial Training', *Occupational Psychology*, **18**, (3), 104–11.

Coopers and Lybrand Associates (1985), *A Challenge to Complacency, changing attitudes to training*, report to the Manpower Services Commission and the National Economic Development Office, London: HMSO.

Downs, S. (1983), 'Industrial Training', in Williams, A.P.O. (ed.), *Using Personnel Research*, Aldershot: Gower.

Glaser, R. (1961), 'Training in Industry', in Karn, H.W. and von Haller-Gilmer, B. (eds), *Readings in Industrial and Business Psychology*, New York: McGraw-Hill, 129–51.

Haire, M. (1952), 'Some Problems of Industrial Training', in Karn, H.W. and von Haller-Gilmer, B. (eds), *Readings In Industrial and Business Psychology*, New York:McGraw-Hill.

Hewitt, A.I.G. (1944), 'Some Aspects of Organised Training', *Occupational Psychology*, **18**, 185–91.

Holding, D.H. (1965), *Principles of Training*, Oxford: Pergamon Press.

Ladhams, G.H. (1952), 'A New Method For Training Operators', *Personnel*, **28**, 471–7.

Lawshe, C.H. (1952), 'Training Operative Personnel', in Karn, H.W. and von Haller-Gilmer, B. (eds), *Readings In Industrial and Business Psychology*, New York: McGraw-Hill.

Lindahl, L.G. (1945), 'Movement Analysis as an Industrial Training Method', *Journal of Applied Psychology*, **29**, 420–36.

McGehee, W. (1949), 'Training In Industry', in Dennis, W., Shartle, C.L., Flanagan, J.C. *et al.*, *Current Trends In Industrial Psychology*, Pittsburgh: University of Pittsburgh Press, 84–114.

McGehee, W. (1952), 'Persistent Problems in Training', in Karn, H.W. and von Haller-Gilmer, B. (eds), *Readings In Industrial and Business Psychology*, New York: McGraw-Hill.

National Institute of Industrial Psychology (1956), *Training Factory Workers*, London: Staples Press.

Pearcey, A.R.H. (1976), 'A Brief Description of Improved Machinist Training', *Bobbin*, September, 62 ff.

Planty, E.G., McCord, W.S. and Efferson, C.A. (1948), *Training Employees and Managers For Production and Teamwork*, New York: The Ronald Press.

Schultz, R.S. and McFarland, R.A. (1935), 'Industrial Psychology in the Soviet Union', *Journal of Applied Psychology*, **19**, 265–308.

Seymour, W.D. (1954), *Industrial Training for Manual Operations*, London: Pitman.

Seymour, W.D. (1979), 'Occupational Psychology through Autobiography: W.D. Seymour', *Journal of Occupational Psychology*, **52**, 241–53.

Viteles, M. (1946), 'War Time Applications of Psychology: Their Value to Industry', *Occupational Psychology*, **20**, (1), 1–20.

Wolfle, D. (1951), 'Training', in Stevens, S.S. (ed.), *Handbook of Experimental Psychology*, New York: Wiley, 1267–86.

2

Training technology

This chapter continues the discussion of the 'training' context into which instruction fits. In it we consider the technology of training, what it is and its relationship to instruction.

There are many definitions of training but, while superficially they seem to differ, underneath they are all very similar. In essence, training is a way of helping people to do things that they could not do before they were trained – and that is the most important aspect of training. If a training course purported to teach you to swim, but at the end of it you could not swim, then training has not finished. It is irrelevant how long you have been in training, how much money has been spent, how many people have been involved or what happened during the training; the simple fact is that if you cannot swim the training is not complete. Training is not about how long a programme lasts or what you do on the programme. Training is about what you can do at the end of training that you could not do before – and it is also about how well you can do it.

Training tends to be formal – that is, it is not something that just happens to the trainee, it is a planned activity to a greater or lesser extent. That means that within a training programme there will be some learning goals to attain, and when those goals are attained you are 'trained'. In between setting the goals and achieving the goals is some form of planned activity that should help you to achieve the goals. Also, training is usually structured – that is, the more basic aspects of the task are learned before the more complicated and difficult parts of the task. Finally, it is usually necessary to have some form of pre-planned measurement going on in training so that the degree of attainment of learning can be assessed. This helps you to control the training process. If progress is too slow then the training can be adjusted to help the trainee learn faster. Also it helps you to make sure that the learning that goes on is what was planned.

Much of training research and literature is concerned with how to span the gap between setting training goals and achieving the goals. It asks the question, 'What should be done and how can we make sure it achieves the goals as quickly as possible?' This subject area, with all of its many aspects and approaches, constitutes what I think of as the 'technology of training'. Let us examine some of the issues involved in making sure the training achieves the goals as quickly and reliably as possible.

The technology of training

Whether the tasks to be mastered by the trainee are sport- or industry-based, academic or practical, the major concern of the trainer is that they are mastered quickly and completely. To help with that aim many trainers have spent many years developing:

- training programmes;
- training manuals and equipment;
- specific exercises to help skill develop or to build necessary physical resources;
- written procedures to codify decision-making processes when working with complex machinery; and
- methods of measuring how effectively all this works so it can be adjusted and improved.

This vast range of techniques and approaches makes up the technology of training. In just the same way that the motor industry has produced a vast range of specialist designers and car makers generating a vast span of different vehicle parts and specifications, the training industry has generated a vast range of technical products. The day-to-day trainer in industry or the sports coach is, basically, equivalent to the motor mechanic in what they do. A motor mechanic will understand how to rebuild and maintain a specific number of motor types and will have a set way of going about each task on each model. A trainer or instructor will also specialize in some areas, they will understand how to develop a range of specific skills for a particular set of tasks and will have a set way of going about each. Both the mechanic and the trainer will need to diagnose and overcome the problems as they go about their profession. Both will be judged by the performance of the finished product!

The whole of the technology of training falls into three major categories:

1. What should the trainee learn? Or, what do we want the trainees to be able to do?
2. How should we go about developing those understandings and behaviours?; or, what is the best training method?
3. After the training, is the trainee doing what we wanted them to do, and if not, why not?

What do we want the trainees to be able to do?

If you are going to design a training programme it is important that the content of training is useful. For example, it is no good designing a programme to develop sales skills and persuasion skills for salespeople if the skills and techniques which are taught don't actually work!

This actually happened to one company (you will remember this from the Preface). For many years successful selling was understood to be due to the way that the salesperson behaved during the selling process; the way that an insurance sales representative, say, described the products to the customer and the way that the customer was invited to buy were taken to be the basis for success. Over many years a set of techniques was developed which was universally believed to be the best way to go about selling. Then, in the early 1970s, a large company selling office equipment (let's call them XYZ Ltd) asked some psychologists to assess the effectiveness of the sales training being carried out by XYZ's training department. Their main concern was that at the end of the training course the trainee sellers should be putting the techniques into practice with their prospective customers – and that, of course, is a valid and quite correct concern for any training programme. In the event, the psychologists found that some of the trainees were putting it into practice and some were not – perhaps the training programme should be improved, then? Clearly, either the instruction or the training methods were not fully effective. But something else was discovered as well.

The psychologists found that the trainee sellers who were putting into practice the techniques they had been taught had the worst sales records of all of the students. In contrast, the trainees who were avoiding the 'traditional' selling techniques and were selling in other ways tended to have better sales results. Clearly there was a problem with the content of the training as well as the training itself. It took a sustained research effort, over several years, on the part of the psychologists before they could describe exactly how successful salespeople went about obtaining sales orders. On the strength of that they went on to design an extremely successful and effective training course which they now market worldwide.

The moral of the story is that the content of the training programme must be correct if the trainees are to be effective in what they must do. That general lesson holds for skills throughout both industry and sport. If the content is valid then the training can proceed. But the next problem is to have training programmes that are well designed so that the trainees have the opportunity to develop their new skill. If the content is not valid and useful then the best programme in the world will not allow the trainees to perform well when it matters.

What is the best training method? Or, how do we design the course?

When the content of training is identified and when you know what outcomes you want the trainees to be able to achieve, you must design the training event that will provide the skills. There are two main areas that have to be considered here: first, you will have to identify what training methods will best develop the skills you want and fit the methods into a sequence that will help the skills to grow; second, there are a range of organizational issues that have to be considered. For example, how many instructors do you need with the design you have chosen, and can you afford them?, What equipment will be needed and what effect will that have on the venue you choose? And so on. Often the organizational problems that would arise from using an ideal training method are so great that second-best training methods must be used instead. So, training programmes are either very expensive (to accommodate the ideal training methods, the special venues needed and the special equipment, etc.) or they are a compromise between the effectiveness of the training methods and the complexity and cost of the training event.

What sort of things have to be considered when designing the best training method? It depends a lot on the nature of the skills that are being developed and the levels of performance that are demanded of the trainees. The nature of the skills will determine the nature of the practice required and that will determine the special equipment that may be needed – for example, some tasks are so complex that special simulators are necessary so that practice can be both carefully controlled and safe (some instances are nuclear power station control rooms, the space shuttle and passenger aircraft flight decks). Other skills are complex in the sense that certain parts must be learned before other parts, hence the skill practice must be carefully structured in the correct sequence if the skills are to develop properly. That is particularly true for unfamiliar skills. Quite often the skills to be learned are based on existing skills being used in unfamiliar ways – for example, the successful selling skills training described earlier is based on the seller asking certain questions of the buyer. The sellers do not really need to be taught how to ask questions or how to phrase questions; they can do that already. What they do need is practice in when to ask certain questions and what to do with the information that comes back. When skills of this sort need to be developed the training programme is often based on practising the old skills in new ways, for example by using role-plays and discussion.

The methods used in training are very important for success but it is easy to choose the wrong method to use when designing training programmes. For example: lecturing does not develop action skills very well but it is very useful for passing over knowledge to large groups of people; it is easy to put practice sessions in the wrong order and try to develop complex skills before the underlying basic skills are well established; or, it is very easy to put too much into a training course so that the trainees become overloaded and awash with new information that they cannot put into practice properly. Unfortunately, although it is very important to choose the right method there are no clear-cut guidelines or underlying principles which trainers can use to design training programmes and training design is therefore always something of a hit-and-miss process. The very best trainers and those with much experience in a certain area will tend to get it more right more often than will less experienced trainers. The very best and the very experienced will also get it wrong from time to time, though.

Familiarity with training approaches for particular skills is a vital factor in successful training design. Most successful training is based on successful training developed elsewhere to develop slightly different skills. Trainers depend on other trainers' experience and approaches. They will usually look to see how something was done elsewhere and will modify it to fit the current need. They will then run the new programme and measure how successful various parts of it were, change them around a bit on subsequent programmes until better results appear and then run the programme in that way. Eventually someone else will borrow the design and apply it to their current training problem, and so it goes. Training evaluation is more often used to modify and design training programmes than it is to assess the usefulness of training for the organizations using it, and that is because most training is grown from existing stock rather than built from predetermined principles.

Why does training fail?

It is useful to think about why training programmes fail because that provides us with some other important influences on the design of effective training. We have already noted that the content of the training has to be correct. Teaching people to do things that do not work is commonplace. Superficially, a training programme or training event can look good, but if the content is flawed then the training is, to all intents and purposes, worthless. But content is not everything. If the training method used is inappropriate or there are unreasonable constraints on the training event (for example, too little time, or far too many trainees) then there is a good chance that little or no useful behaviour change will occur. Once again, the training is worthless. It also makes sense to ponder the possibility that a good content and a good programme design can be inadvertently sabotaged by a totally useless instructor. That is the subject of the rest of the book so we will not go into that in detail at the moment. Suffice it to say that what the instructor tries to do when instructing effectively and how the instructor goes about instructing effectively are not immediately obvious. With an understanding of the trainee's built-in system of skill acquisition and a few research findings, however, the process of instruction suddenly becomes fairly straightforward and obvious.

We can fit the three training factors we have discussed into a training triangle (Figure 2.1).

The effectiveness of a training programme or training event depends on these three aspects: the validity of the training content, the appropriateness of the training methods and the quality of instruction that occurs on the programme. Many programmes which superficially look good in one of the areas could be poor in one or both of the other areas. So, the wise user of training services will ask for evidence that the training programme works. Good trainers will understand the principles of evaluation of training and will apply them to show both that their training programme is effective in developing the skills it is meant to develop and that the skills which are being developed are the right ones for the task to be performed.

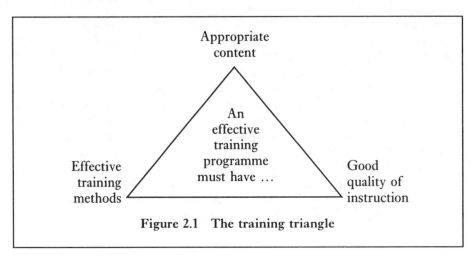

Figure 2.1   The training triangle

There are several other problems with training that have to be examined by training evaluation. In the real world having a good training programme with all the three triangle factors working well does not guarantee that the trainees will apply the skills when the training is finished. It is true that many training programmes are poor because the training triangle is faulty, but it is also true that many training programmes are ineffective because the organization to which the trainees return after training is not equipped to allow the new skills to be used. So, what was the point in training them if they cannot use their new skills?

Are the trainees able to do what we want them to do?

Training evaluation is concerned with measuring the effectiveness of training. Evaluation grew out of academic research (because that is often concerned with how to measure events) and was first applied widely in military training. It was only in the 1960s that training evaluation methods became a regular and important part of training technology. Many books, articles and professional training programmes acknowledge the importance of evaluation to good training practice. Unfortunately no more than lip service is often paid to evaluation; current surveys and official research make it clear that evaluation is not widely used by most trainers in the UK and in the USA. When we have considered what evaluation is about we will have completed our review of the background to training.

The most quoted model of how to evaluate originated with an article by Kirkpatrick in 1959. According to this model four items should be measured if training effectiveness is to be adequately assessed:

1. The participant's reactions to the training – did they enjoy it, did they think it was relevant and interesting? Most training courses ask such questions but on their own they are not very important. It is more useful to

measure if the participants learned something from the training and that is what the other three points discuss.

2. The participant's learning – during and after the training find out how well the training content was assimilated by the participants. This tells you something about the training methods used.

3. Behaviour change – what behaviour changes occurred as a result of the training? Training is about changing behaviour. If behaviour does not change then the training is ineffective and needs a serious redesign – or a better instructor!

4. Organizational results – what changes in organizational variables (for example, changes in costs, productivity and turnover) have resulted? After all, this is why most industrial training is undertaken: to improve the way things are done. A good training programme may produce learning and behaviour change on the course but fail to produce the same effect back on the job. The transfer of learning from the training programme to the workplace is just as important as the training itself.

Many trainers are familiar with this model. Although Kirkpatrick's model says what should be measured, however, it does not say how to measure. More recent authors (for example, Warr *et al.* and Hamblin) have tried to help trainers by outlining how to measure training effectiveness. They suggest that several areas should be assessed for effective evaluation. First, there should be some planning to identify what the training is intended to achieve. You should think about the training objectives under some or all of the areas given in Table 2.1.

Table 2.1   Evaluating training, stage 1: set your training objectives

- Reaction objectives: what reactions to the training do you want the trainees to have? Do you want them to think it relevant, useful, fun, challenging, difficult, horrific, just like work – or something else?
- Learning objectives: how knowledgeable should trainees be at the end of training? What do you want them to know?
- Job behaviour objectives: what changes in job behaviour are desired? What should they be able to do after the training that they cannot do before training? This area is very important and how you answer the question is important too. Do not answer it in a vague way ('They should be better at communication after the training'); instead, be specific (for example: 'After the training they should be: asking more questions', 'summarizing more often in meetings', 'making more positive suggestions', and so on).
- Organization objectives: what effect on the organization should the training produce? Some of these outcomes are directly measurable (for example, more sales, increased productivity, less waste, etc.), some outcomes are less directly measurable. Wherever possible try to have some measurable outcomes.
- Ultimate value objectives: what is the long-term value to the organization that is required?

Clearly, different training tasks will require objectives to be set in some rather than all of these areas. For example, training an individual for a sporting event will probably mean that the organizational objectives in Table 2.1 are replaced with some outcomes of a more personal nature. After you have decided the outcomes you want to achieve you must design the training and run the training event. During and after the training you should measure the outcomes that are achieved in the areas shown in Table 2.2. (There are lots of ways to measure these items and there are books to help you measure them; at the moment we are just outlining the main areas to be measured.)

It is worth emphasizing that the purpose of training evaluation is to improve the training itself. To do this three things must be undertaken: the training objectives must be set; the methods of gathering information must be established; and the information collected must be compared to the objectives. The training process is then readjusted as necessary to meet objectives, or the objectives themselves are changed.

Table 2.2   Evaluating training, stage 2: measuring the outcomes of training

- Reaction effects: trainee reactions to the training – what do they think about the training and is that what you wanted them to think? What are the implications for the design and delivery of the training?
- Learning effects: what knowledge learning occurred and was it appropriate? What are the implications for the design and delivery of the training?
- Job behaviour effects: what changes in job behaviour occurred? This is probably the most important area as it this which determines what they will do differently after the training. Unfortunately it is also the area least likely to be assessed. Most training asks for trainee reactions (in the infamous training course 'smiles sheets' that trainees are asked to fill in after the programme finishes) and ignores the other areas of assessment.
- Organization effects: what organizational effects resulted from the training? This is important for industrial and commercial training as it is the reason why the training is carried out in the first place. It is, however, seldom assessed. In sport this is likely to be associated with team performance – what effect did training have on an individual's or a team's performance?
- Ultimate value effects: what ultimate value to the organization or team was realized? In industry and commerce the ultimate utility of the training to the organization is in financial terms – this is termed a utility analysis. In utility analysis a distinction is drawn between a cost–benefit analysis (where training cost in financial terms is compared to non-financial benefits arising such as attitude changes or safety improvements) and cost-effectiveness analysis (where monetary training costs are compared with financial payoffs to the organization such as increased production or less wastage and scrap).

Summary

Let us briefly review the points made so far. Training technology is concerned with the methods of training to produce a result. It involves finding out what contributes to effective performance of the task (whether that is a sport task or an industrial task) and thus determines the content of training. Training technology determines the methods of training and developing those skills. It then goes on to look at the impact the training has on the organization. An important part of training technology is concerned with measuring the effectiveness of training. That is important because it helps trainers to improve the process of training. Training technology is therefore important and necessary because it provides, as it were, the playing field in which the instructor can play the instructional game with the trainee. Training technology helps you, the instructor, to do your job but it is not more important than your job. Without an instructor putting it all into practice the training technology is worthless. The whole of the technology stands or falls on how well the instructor does his or her job.

I have already noted that wherever possible the content of this book is based on research rather than opinion. I suggested that this was a good thing because it helps us to avoid the pitfalls associated with following the personal opinion or prejudices of others. There is a good deal of research that is relevant to the technology of training – for example, psychological research on skill acquisition and performance growth, training research on how well given approaches to training will develop skill, and so on. If the technology of training stands or falls on the effectiveness of the individual instructor then, to be consistent, we should be convinced that instructors are useful and necessary in the training process, and one problem with that is the lack of research which explores the importance of the instructor as a serious research topic. The investigations that do explore this topic are rare and were mostly performed in the very early years of the development of training technology. Nevertheless in the next chapter we will look at just how important instructors are to the training process.

Bibliography

Training research and theory

Campbell, J.P. (1971), 'Personnel Training and Development', *Annual Review of Psychology*, **22**, 565–602.

Goldstein, I.L. (1980), 'Training in Work Organisations', *Annual Review of Psychology*, **31**, 229–72.

Goldstein, I.L. (1986), *Training in Organisations: Needs Assessment, Development, and Evaluation*, 2nd edn, Pacific Grove, CA: Brooks/Cole.

Goldstein, I.L. and Gessner, M.J. (1988), 'Training and Development in Work Organisations', in Cooper, C.L. and Robertson, I.T., *International Review of Industrial and Organisational Psychology*, Chichester: John Wiley and Sons.
Latham, G.P. (1988), 'Human Resource Training and Development', *Annual Review of Psychology*, 39, 545–82.
Morrison, J.E. (ed.) (1991), *Training For Performance, Principles of Applied Human Learning*, London: John Wiley and Sons.
Patrick, J. (1992), *Training: Research and Practice*, London: Academic Press.
Wexley, K.N. (1984), 'Personnel Training', *Annual Review of Psychology*, 35, 519–51.

Training practice

Bass, B.M. and Vaughan, J.A. (1966), *Training in Industry: the management of learning*, Monterey, CA: Brooks/Cole; London: Tavistock Publications.
Davies, I.K. (1971), *The Management of Learning*, London: McGraw-Hill.
Deloitte Haskins and Sells/IFF Research Ltd. (1989), *Training in Britain: Employers Activities*, London: HMSO.
Hinrichs, J.R. (1976), 'Personnel Training', in Dunnette, M.D. (ed.), *Handbook of Industrial and Organisational Psychology*, Chicago: Rand McNally College Publishing Company, 829–60.

Designing training programmes

Campbell, C.P. (1987), 'Instructional Systems Development: A Methodology for Vocational–Technical Training', *Journal of European Industrial Training*, 11, (5), (monograph).
Gagne, R.M. and Briggs, L.J. (1974), *Principles of Instructional Design*, London: Holt, Rhinehart and Winston.
Goldstein, I.L. (1986), *Training in Organisations: Needs Assessment, Development, and Evaluation*, 2nd edn, Pacific Grove, CA: Brooks/Cole.
Hamblin, A.C. (1974), *Evaluation and Control of Training*, London: McGraw-Hill.
Kirkpatrick, F.H. (1959), 'Techniques for evaluating training programs', *Journal of the American Society of Training Directors*, 13, 3–9, 21–6.
Romiszowski, A.J. (1968), *The Selection and Use of Teaching Aids*, London: Kogan Page.
Romiszowski, A. J. (1981), *Designing Instructional Systems, Decision Making in Course Planning and Curriculum Design*, New York: Kogan Page; London: Nichols Publishing.
Warr, P., Bird, M. and Rackham, N. (1970), *Evaluation of Management Training*, Aldershot: Gower Press.

Further reading

Hamblin, A.C. (1974), *Evaluation and Control of Training*, London: McGraw-Hill.

Harrison, R. (1988), *Training and Development*, London: Institute of Personnel Management.

Jinks, M. (1979), *Training*, Poole: Blandford Press.

Kenney, J. and Reid, M. (1988), *Training Interventions*, 2nd edn, London: Institute of Personnel Management.

King, D. (1964), *Training Within the Organisation: a study of company policy and procedures for the systematic training of operators and supervisors*, London: Tavistock Publications.

Morgan, T. and Costello, M. (1984), *Trainer Task Inventory*, London: Manpower Services Commission and Institute of Training and Development.

National Coaching Foundation (1986), *The Coach at Work*, Leeds: National Coaching Foundation.

Spoor, J., Bennet, R. and Leduchowiz, T. (1984), *Guide to Trainer Effectiveness*, London: Manpower Services Commission and Institute of Training and Development.

Training In Britain: A Study of Funding, Activity and Attitudes (1989), London: HMSO.

3

Are instructors useful?

Given the fact that every training programme has an instructor, we might expect that the role and the impact of the instructor on the training would be well researched and understood, but that is not the case. So, do we really need instructors at all? Just how useful are they? This chapter reviews the evidence.

The instructor is the most visible part of training to the participants. For many trainees the instructor is the person who, in a very real sense, 'gives' them their skills and knowledge. There has been a lot of research and development in training generally, so we might expect that there would be as much research asking how useful instructors are. Are they just the public face of training or are they an integral part of the training process? Surprisingly, in the past 70 years there have been but a handful of investigations that have tried to answer that question.

The few investigations that have been carried out fall into two main camps: one group of studies asks the basic question 'Does the presence of instructors speed or enhance the training process?' and a second group of studies asks whether particular techniques of training speed or enhance training and, in doing this, indirectly investigates the impact of the skills that the instructor brings to the training. Both groups of investigations have examined instructors in industry and in sport. Let us see what they found. We will consider group one studies first.

Do instructors speed or enhance training?

There have not been many serious investigations which ask whether having an instructor present and active is more useful than having no instructor. Perhaps the earliest important research was some laboratory-based research carried out in 1925, which concluded that:

- instruction reduced the number of practice attempts needed to master the learning task in the vast majority of cases;
- instruction had most effect early in the learning process and its effectiveness appeared to decrease later on in learning;
- instruction operated to reduce the number of errors made during the learning period;
- positive guidance and error correction by the instructors was very helpful to the trainees.

Under laboratory conditions, therefore, instructors definitely help trainee skills to develop. The instructors helped the process by correcting errors and telling the trainees what to do.

Other researchers (in 1929) moved out of the laboratory into the schools to discover how helpful instruction could be in teaching children a throwing task. They found that uncontrolled practice was a 'relatively uncertain' way of acquiring skill. When the children practised throwing using a constant method of throwing, however, they were more likely to improve their throwing accuracy. If the instructors made verbal suggestions and criticized the children following each throw but did not encourage the use of a fixed method of throwing the children did not improve. Thus the instructor also has a role in making sure that a constant method is used for the task to be learned.

From quite an early time, then, there has been research evidence that instructors are helpful to people learning a new skill. More than that, instructors had to be doing certain things if they were to be a positive help. They have to tell trainees what to do, correct errors and make sure the trainee practises one method of doing the task. We must assume that if the instructor is to carry out those activities effectively he or she should know the methods to be used by the trainee and must know them in advance. If that pre-knowledge is not there the instructor cannot tell the trainee what to do and cannot correct errors. Most research after these early studies developed these themes and enriched the picture across a range of instructional situations. One study investigated instruction in archery, another investigated children's throwing again, a third examined athletics practice and a fourth and fifth investigated the effects of instructors in industry. They all found that having an instructor present either improved the rate of skill development (that is, they cut the training time) or improved the standard of skill obtained, or both. In addition, they all found that the important factor was what the instructor did when present. Just standing and watching was not enough. The instructor had to be instructing as the trainee performed. In summary, these studies found that:

- having instructors present improves skill development – it is faster when they are present;
- the instructor aids the learner by directing his or her attention to more adequate techniques than those being employed;
- when trainees were asked to practise an industrial task at maximum speed with systematic instruction 'on points to be observed in manipulating the

material' they produced a superior performance over a group required to practise at speed with no instruction;

- new workers in a textile factory trained by trained instructors had higher levels of productivity at the end of the training period than did trainees trained by skilled workers.

The research shows the importance of proper instruction to the acquisition of skill. When no instructor is present, then the skill tends not to develop as quickly or to as high a level as when the instructor is present. There is more to instruction than just having someone present, however: don't forget, having trained instructors present produces better results than having skilled workers present. The instructor must also be doing instructional activities – directing and correcting movements and, by implication, identifying best movement patterns in advance so that he or she can ensure the trainees use only the effective movements. That brings us to the second group of investigations into instruction. These investigate the effect of the instructor's skill on the process of skill development.

The instructor's skill and the trainee's skill development

We have seen in the examples above that it is not enough to just have someone there when trainees are learning a new skill. That someone must be doing certain things if the trainee is to develop the skill quickly. Between the 1940s and the 1980s instructor research tried to find out what instructors should be doing and when they should be doing it. The details of the research findings are described in much more detail in later chapters. The investigators found that instructors, just like their trainees, could be skilled to varying degrees. It was not just *what* instructors did, although that is very important. It became clear that *how* the instructor did it and *when* the instructor did it were also very important aspects of the instructor's skill. If there wasn't time to apply the full range of instructional skills – for example, if there were too many trainees to instruct – then the instructor could not expect very good results. For example, one industrial study found that when a skilled instructor trained one unskilled trainee that trainee achieved required standards on the task in just under three weeks. However, each additional trainee that the instructor had to deal with added three weeks to the overall training time. So, when the instructor had to train three trainees at once the overall training time rose from three weeks to over nine weeks. Additional trainees dilute the application of the instructor's skill and that dramatically slows the rate of skill development.

The various research strands show that an instructor with a narrow range of instructing techniques available will be, on average, likely to obtain worse results than one with a wider range of instructing techniques available. An instructor able to apply a wide range of techniques will be successful only if he or she can apply them effectively, and the skills needed in order to do that were found to be rather subtle. Finally, if the instructor does not apply those skills at the correct stage of skill development then the trainee will not develop the skills as rapidly as possible.

This latter point is very important. The instructor is at the mercy of the trainee's learning processes. It is not possible to install a skill into the trainee's mind. It can only be taken in by the trainee actively trying to learn it. So the instructor is helping the trainee to learn quickly by removing potential blocks that might prevent the learning taking place. That means the instructor is reacting to the trainee and the trainee is reacting to the instruction – the process of instruction is a dance between the trainee and the instructor, as intimate and as complex as a tango.

Summary

The research that has been carried out shows clearly that:

- Trainees who receive no instruction either do not gain skill or gain skill very slowly. The presence of an instructor can cut training times considerably.
- It is not enough to have an instructor present. The instructor must be doing certain instructing activities if trainees are to gain their skills as rapidly as possible. When the instructor has to deal with many trainees the effect is to dilute the instructor's skill and slow the skill development.

If we want to instruct well we must understand how trainees develop skill. I will describe that in later chapters. Before moving on to consider what happens to the trainee when they develop skill, let us pull together the research and development findings. The next chapter will sketch an outline of the what and how of instruction. We will cover the when in a later chapter.

Bibliography

Cox, J. (1933), 'Some Experiments on Formal Training in the Acquisition of Skill', *British Journal of Psychology*, 24, 67–87.

Davies, D.R. (1945), 'The Effect of Tuition upon the Process of Learning a Complex Motor Skill', *Journal of Experimental Psychology*, 36, 352–65.

Dusenberry, L. (1952), 'A Study of the Effects of Training in Ball Throwing by Children Aged Three to Seven', *The Research Quarterly*, 23, 9–14.

Flegg, D. (1983), 'Developing Instructor Effectiveness – the P.O.I.S.E. approach', *Personnel Management*, May, 38–40.

Flegg, D., Warren, A. and Law, C. (1982), *POISE: Project On Instructor Style and Effectiveness*, Cambridge: Industrial Training Research Unit Ltd.

Florjancic, J. (1968), 'On-the-job Training and Its Practical Usefulness', *Poklicno Usmerjanje*, 11–12, 276–80.

Goodenough, F.L. and Brian, C.R. (1929), 'Certain Factors Underlying the Acquisition of Motor Skill by Pre-school Children', *Journal of Experimental Psychology*, **XII**, 127–55.

James, R. (1989), *The Influence of Skilled Instructors and Numbers of Trainees upon the Rate of Acquisition of Sewing Skills*, unpublished paper to the Conference of the Occupational Division and Section of the British Psychological Society, Bowness-on-Windermere, January.

James, R. (1993), *The development of a systems based heuristic to guide practice in the training of industrial manual skills*, unpublished PhD thesis, University of Hull.

Pearcey, A.R.H. (1976), 'A Brief Description of Improved Machinist Training', *Bobbin*, September, 62 ff.

Seymour, W. D. (1959), 'Training Operatives in Industry', *Ergonomics*, **2**, (2), 143–47.

Seymour, W.D. (1968), *Skills Analysis Training*, London: Pitman.

Wang, T.L. (1925), 'The Influence of Tuition in the Acquisition of Skill', *Psychological Monographs*, **34**, (1).

Whilden, P.P. (1956), 'Comparison of Two Methods of Teaching Beginning Basketball', *The Research Quarterly*, **27**, (2), 235–42.

4

The instructional process

You, as instructor, are not just the public face of the training programme, you are an important and fundamental part of the programme. The evidence I have cited in Chapter 3 shows that when instructors are not present the trainees do not develop their skills as quickly as when instructors are present. So it is you, the instructor, at centre stage rather than the training technology that you use. Skill development is a dance between you and the trainee, the training technology is the music to which you both move. In this section we will try to find out the steps of the instructional dance – what do you do when you instruct effectively?

General agreement about the process of instruction developed initially from the need to train industrial instructors during the period of the Second World War when a male workforce was replaced with a female workforce (and vice versa as the war ended). Many of the recommendations were developed in the USA and came into the UK as the Training Within Industry (or TWI) programme (Table 4.1).

Table 4.1   The TWI framework

Show workers how to do it.
Explain key points.
Let them watch you do it again.
Let them do the simple parts of the job.
Help them to do the whole job.
Let them do the whole job but watch them.

This framework is summarized in a variety of well-known and similar acronyms, all of which are designed to be easy to remember. For example, the UK armed forces encapsulate the instruction process as EDIT. This represents:

- Explain.
- Demonstrate.
- Instruct (coach).
- Test performance.

An alternative version is the Tell, Show, Do summary of instruction. As simple mnemonics designed to be used by people who must instruct but who are not primarily instructors such devices as TWI, EDIT and Tell-Show-Do may be useful. They summarize what the instructor should do but they say nothing about how to go about doing those things most effectively.

An underlying foundation of all of these approaches is that the instructor understands the task to be learned sufficiently well to be able to show and explain as well as know what to watch for (TWI point 6) as the trainee performs. To help this understanding develop the TWI scheme of instructor training also included a rough-and-ready method of looking at a task and breaking it down into its component parts – a form of task analysis. A very well known form of instructor training in industry in the 1950s and 1960s was based on this analysis of task requirements and came to be known as skills analysis training. However, although skills analysis training was very influential and widely applied, it focused on breaking down and analysing the task to be taught but said little or nothing about how to instruct when the analysis was completed. There can be great value in undertaking task analysis insofar as the instructor who understands the task is able to perceive aspects of the task which the trainee cannot. Hence, the instructor must be aware of those hidden aspects and must help the trainee with those tricky bits until he or she gains sufficient skill to do it for themselves.

As understanding of the instructor's task developed the descriptions of the process of instruction grew more sophisticated. The what was expanded to include the pre-training analysis of the task and some of the how began to be included. If we put some of these descriptions together we produce the outline of instruction shown in Table 4.2.

That is a much better description of the process of instruction, but it is still very what-oriented and not very how-focused – that is, it lists what instructors do but does not explain how to do it effectively. This is particularly important because the research that followed the development of this scheme was concerned with the how and discovered that the how of instruction was as important as the what sequence described in Table 4.2. This book is particularly concerned with fitting the two aspects of instruction together to produce a complete description of instruction which you can take away with you to improve the way you go about instructing. What is missing from the above model? Recent research has found two very important additional factors that greatly multiply the effectiveness of instruction.

First, the way in which the instructor corrects errors is of overwhelming importance, so much so that if weekend instructors (say, an amateur gymnastics coach or football coach) were to adopt nothing else but an effective style of error correction their trainees' performance, confidence and motivation to

---

Table 4.2   A first description of the instructor's task

1. Analyse the job – the steps in the operation, key points to know, key points to watch out for, common tricks of the trade that help experienced workers perform the task, safety factors, care of machines and quality standards.
2. Preparation – prepare lesson plan, materials, visual aids, workplace layout, targets, demonstration, equipment.
3. Prepare the workplace – clean and care for equipment, prepare workplace layout.
4. Present or show task to the trainee.
5. Instruct:

   - prepare the trainee, check existing knowledge, put trainee at ease;
   - present the operation, gain and maintain the trainee's attention, instructor to tell and show stressing key points, knacks, safety and quality standards. Instructor to perform job as trainee instructs or instructor to question trainee to check for understanding. Instructor to remedy any knowledge deficit as necessary;
   - allow the trainee to perform but stop when mistakes are made – instructor supervises until performance correct, corrects errors, checks work output, gives feedback immediately;
   - put trainee to work – explain personal responsibilities, identify sources of help, arrange follow-up;
   - follow up initial instruction to act as a source of help and to ensure that best methods are adhered to.

---

train would improve dramatically. We will explain these techniques in detail in Chapters 14 and 15.

Second, instructing research has found that the instructor *must* match what he or she says and does to the particular stage of skill development that the trainee has currently achieved. There is a pattern of instructing, the tempo of which is set by the trainee's skill growth. When the instructor ignores the pattern and does what he or she wants, when he or she wants to do it, then the trainee's skill does not develop! Why? Because the trainee is the centre, the focus, of instructional effort and sets the instructional agenda. Instructors ignore that at their peril. This point is explained in more detail in the next two chapters.

Everything the instructor does should be designed to help the trainee's skill development processes function effectively. It is the trainee who is learning and the trainee who is developing skill. We cannot do it for them. Skills will develop only when trainees try to perform them – doing the task and skill growth go together. An instructor may try to help us do that as effectively as possible, but that is all they can do – help. And some instructors are more helpful than others. The skill development process working inside each of us sets the tempo which the training process has to match. If the training process and the instructional process do not help our internal learning processes we will not learn what we are supposed to learn. In the instructional dance, the trainee leads and the instructor follows.

Summary

This chapter has outlined three aspects of instructing: *what* must be done during instruction, *how* to do the various aspects of instructing and *when* to do the various aspects of instructing. All three of these points must be addressed by anyone wishing to instruct effectively. It is not enough to list *what* to do, the instructor must also be clear about *how* to do it and *when* to do it. The rest of the book begins to develop these points in more detail.

The next chapter describes our internal processes of skill development from the point of view of the instructor. It describes what happens when we learn skills and explains what instructors can do to help that process along. Later chapters describe the instructor's toolkit and how to use it for honing the trainee's skill development to the maximum possible efficiency.

Bibliography

Haire, M. (1952), 'Some Problems of Industrial Training', in Karn, H.W. and von Haller-Gilmer, B. (eds), *Readings In Industrial and Business Psychology*, New York: McGraw-Hill.

Jinks, M. (1979), *Training*, Poole: Blandford Press.

Lawshe, C.H. (1952), 'Training Operative Personnel', in Karn, H.W. and von Haller-Gilmer, B. (eds), *Readings In Industrial and Business Psychology*, New York: McGraw-Hill.

Lindahl, L.G. (1945), 'Movement Analysis as an Industrial Training Method', *Journal of Applied Psychology*, 29, 420–36.

McGehee, W. (1949), 'Training In Industry', in Dennis, W., Shartle, C.L., Flanagan, J.C. *et al.*, *Current Trends In Industrial Psychology*, Pittsburgh: University of Pittsburgh Press, 84–114.

McGehee, W. (1952), 'Persistent Problems in Training', in Karn, H.W. and von Haller-Gilmer, B. (eds), *Readings In Industrial and Business Psychology*, New York: McGraw-Hill.

Planty, E.G., McCord, W.S. and Efferson, C.A. (1948), *Training Employees and Managers For Production and Teamwork*, New York: The Ronald Press Company.

Seymour, W.D. (1954), *Industrial Training for Manual Operations*, London: Pitman.

Seymour, W.D. (1979), 'Occupational Psychology through Autobiography: W. D. Seymour', *Journal of Occupational Psychology*, 52, 241–53.

Viteles, M. (1946), 'War Time Applications of Psychology: Their Value to Industry', *Occupational Psychology*, 20, (1), 1–20.

5

The learning machine

The purpose of this book is to show you how to harness the power of the trainee's learning machine. The way you set up the training and the way that you go about instructing will either help or hinder the automatic learning system. Do not be in any doubt about this – if you are to be an effective instructor you must fit in with the trainee's learning machine and its method of operating. It simply is not possible for the learning machine to fit in with you. This chapter and the next will show you how the trainee's learning machine works and what you must do help it work properly.

Human beings differ from other animals in many ways. For example, we do not have feathers and we cannot breathe under water without special equipment. Body differences such as these have developed over many millions of years to help animal species to live comfortably in different environments. We have a body design specialized for living on land. Nevertheless, unlike many other land animals our body design is also surprisingly non-specialized in most ways. For example, we do not have the claws and sharp teeth of meat-eating hunters but nor do we have the huge crushing teeth and special guts of grazing animals – instead, we can eat most things. Although the human body is relatively non-specialized physically that does not mean to say that we are not specialized in other ways, ways that help us to live almost where we want to – including the moon!

So, if we do not have a body built to fit a specialist animal lifestyle, how are we different to other animals? The answer is that we are the learning specialists of the animal world. Every human being is a powerful learning machine from birth – in fact our childhood is very long compared to that of other animals (even our closest animal relatives) to allow us to learn all the things we need to know to be fully human. But we continue to learn as adults. Our parents and grandparents, our playmates, our workmates all talk to us and show us new things and we remember what they said and did. So powerful is our need to learn that we have invented ways in which people long dead can teach us through stories, books and films.

As babies we learn how to talk and share ideas with others, as toddlers we start to learn all the rules of behaviour that we must know if we are to be accepted by the people around us. At play we practise doing 'grown up' things and we learn how to work our bodies effectively. At school we start to learn technical knowledge to help us manipulate the world around us. Some of the learning we do is formal in nature – lessons, lectures, demonstrations and so on. Most of it we do not even know is happening because, for us, everyday life shows us new things and new ways of behaving and we absorb it all without even thinking about it. We store new information, facts and feelings through-out our lifetime. We are like information sponges, soaking up new things and storing them all in our brain's memory system.

It is the automatic system in our brains that helps us to absorb knowledge and skill. Any small child demonstrates the effectiveness of the human learning machine – children learn to walk and run, they learn to throw stones, and what to throw them at. Small children learn how to hold babies by imitating the actions of those around them, when they play they practise the actions they see around them. Children learn language and the rules of conversation. They soak them up from the people around them and, given enough time, they become fully skilled adults as a result. Figure 5.1 summarizes the learning machine's main functions.

This learning machine is a wonderful thing to be born with. The amount and variety of experience that humans learn and pass on from generation to generation is amazing – and it is all because of the learning machine inside us. But for instructors trying to teach someone a skill there is a dark side to this powerful, automatic learning machine which we have. The very fact that human learning is powerful and fast can cause some problems, both for the learner and the instructor. We will discuss the problems later on, but for now we will note that much of instruction is about how to avoid those difficulties and how to harness the power of the learning engine that is inside every trainee and learner.

Knowledge and action – two very different things

First let us think about what it is that we learn. Most instructors and teachers agree that, broadly, we learn two things: knowledge and actions. The two tend to be very separate areas of learning requiring different training approaches if we are to get the best result. For example, if I were to organize a lecture for you on how to play the piano it is not very likely that after it you would then be able to go off and play a recognizable tune – despite having knowledge about piano playing you could not perform the necessary actions. Similarly, if I were to arrange a visit to a swimming gala for a group of non-swimmers we would not expect them to be able to swim as a result of seeing a demonstration of others swimming. They might have gained some knowledge about swimming as a result of seeing others swim but it would not necessarily help them to

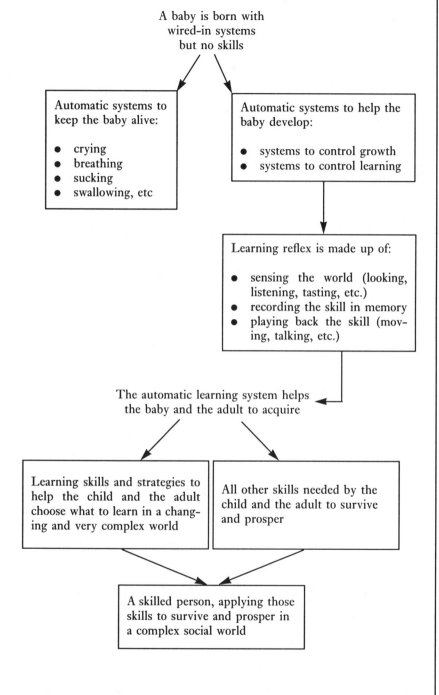

Figure 5.1   The automatic learning system

perform the skilled actions of swimming. Indeed, if our non-swimmers have not been explicitly told what to look at and what to remember about the swimmers we cannot even be sure that they will have collected useful knowledge from their observation of the swimmers in action.

Knowledge on its own does not necessarily help you to act in a skilled fashion. We learn how to *do* by doing rather than by being told. So, when we want someone to develop a skill we must arrange that they learn by doing the skill or parts of it. That may sound like an obvious thing to say, but many instructors set up demonstrations for their trainees and then expect that the trainees will be able to do what they have just seen demonstrated. Unfortunately it does not work like that very often.

Of course, every practical skill has a knowledge component to it. The training programme must arrange for the necessary knowledge to be passed on as well as arranging practice sessions at the activity itself. The point is that you must not expect skilled actions to follow a lecture or a talk or a demonstration. Many instructors and coaches are surprised, or even slightly hurt and offended, that a careful demonstration on their part does not produce instant skilled action by the trainee. The trainees cannot help it, it is not deliberate – demonstration provides only a form of knowledge about a task, it won't produce adequate performance on that task. Adequate performance will only come from the trainee doing it and re-doing it (with appropriate guidance) until it goes smoothly – and the process by which the skill develops means that there is a very good chance that it will go wrong for the trainee. So the role of the instructor is to help the trainee to do it right as often as possible. Then the automatic learning system will record only the right actions.

'But I can't learn – I'm stupid!'

Despite having a very effective and automatic learning machine built into their heads, many people feel that, personally, they are incompetent at learning. It is sad to hear intelligent and able women working as production line supervisors explain how 'thick' or 'stupid' they are. Men with a sound working knowledge of genetics gained from pigeon breeding worry about having to help their children with homework because 'I'm thick.' Why is this? One reason that people feel incompetent at learning is that they remember failure and they remember all the times it was difficult to get it right. In particular, they remember failure when attempting to learn skills valued by society – academic skills, athletic skills and craft skills.

Sometimes poor teaching, or instructing, is to blame for the focus on failure – when an instructor teaches an action skill by lecturing or solely by demonstration it is almost certain that the learner will fail at the task. The poor trainee may take away the idea that she is stupid because she could not do it, or he may have been told by the instructor that he was no good. Instructors are in a powerful position. It is easy to destroy a trainee's confidence and help them to label themselves as incompetent and thick. One of the most powerful tools available to the instructor, therefore, is focusing on the successes achieved by the trainee. Giving trainees powerful and accurate information about how they are progressing can be almost dramatically effective – one instructor who used the feedback techniques described in Chapters 14 and 15 complained that she was having difficulty keeping up with her trainees' rapid progress, she wanted to know how to get them to stop work and go home at the end of the shift!

Taking the learning machine to bits

Millions of years of evolution have provided us with a very powerful ability to learn. We are probably better at learning than any animal that has ever existed. That ability is really several separate parts working together to produce the total learning effect. Some parts of the learning system which we possess as adults were with us when we were born; they are built into our nervous system. The parts of the learning system we were born with probably cannot be changed by us as trainers – we cannot speed them up or make them work in different ways. Some parts of the learning machine are not built-in, they are acquired as we grow – we learn the skills of how to learn. Let us explore the 'wired-in' learning circuits before going on to the learning skills we find for ourselves.

Learning skills we are born with

The human brain is a vastly complex and wonderful living thing that we can think of as a machine. Parts of our brain machine grow themselves just as plants do and, like plants, those parts grow into shapes and patterns that are similar between different individuals. The reason for this is that those parts of the brain control functions that must operate properly if we are to survive. For example, the parts of our brain controlling breathing must grow and work per-fectly from a very early age. The parts of our brain that control the hormone systems must grow and work properly in all of us. So, those parts of our brain that control staying alive probably grow to a genetic plan that determines their structure very carefully – it is the only way to make sure that each of us works properly.

Other parts of our brain must grow according to the experiences we have in life. It just is not possible to grow a brain complete with the full range of memories, skills, facts and words that we all need if we are to cope with the full complexity of our changing world. Our brain is built to get around this problem quite cleverly. It has a built-in system for growing and forming itself in a very flexible manner. Through the operation of these two systems each of us ends up with a brain that is partly pre-built and partly built by ourselves and the world we have experienced. Our personal learning machine is also partly built-in from the start and partly something we acquire for ourselves as we go through life.

We have some systems that are built- in – wired into our brains – that help us to learn some skills. A child's ability to learn language may be something that is part of the way in which our brain is built. That in-built language recorder and player makes it very easy for very young children to learn languages just from hearing them being spoken. The language machine does not come with the words to be used; instead it provides the infant with a strong interest in other people's speech, a set of rules for storing words so that they can be found in memory and a set of rules for generating sentences. It is a general language machine that builds on the language that we hear being used around us.

It would be impossible to have a learning system built into our heads to help us learn every skill that could possibly be invented by all humans across the whole of history and the future. The learning machines that we are born with are those which will help us gain skills that are vital to our survival as a species of animal. The ability to use language seems to be one of these vital survival skills that merit their own special learning machine.

The ability to learn is also a vital survival skill for us as a species of animal. That ability is probably made up of several built-in sets of behaviour that we all share. These built-in behaviours work in such a way as to make sure that we see skills being practised by other people. For example, most people are insatiably curious. We all want to know what is going on and why. Children especially seek out and are attracted by new sights and sounds. That built-in interest ensures that our attention is attracted to what is going on and that focus of attention, of course, gives us a chance to learn something new. A second part of the built-in learning system we all possess is the ability to imitate what other people do. We are attracted to other people and we go where they are. Not only that, when we are with them we watch what they do. Added to this is a powerful desire to copy what they do and the way in which we see them do it. This is especially true of children, but it is also true of adults. This does not refer to our consciously imitating other people, although we do that from time to time. It refers to the imitation that we do not actually notice we are doing – for example, psychologists know very well that when a group of people stand at the side of the road waiting to cross, it only takes one of the group to look as if she is about to cross and the others will tend to start to cross as well. In a singles bar it's easy to identify the couples that will stay together for the evening – they sit in positions that shut out the rest of the room and then they begin to copy each other's movements. When one takes a drink, the other takes a drink. When he crosses his legs, then so will she. Imitation works in reverse as well – if he takes a drink and falls writhing to the floor, it is a safe bet that she will not take a drink from the same glass!

Our learning system tries to set us up so we can learn from what is happening around us. It cannot tell us what to learn, it can only increase the possibility that we will learn something useful from other people. This is the learning mechanism that you, as instructors, cannot hope to change. Instead, you have to work with it. If you can work with it then the trainee's learning will proceed at its natural, very rapid, pace – and that is your role as instructor. Unfortunately, the automatic learning machine seldom operates to its full effectiveness when we want it to. There are a whole host of factors that act to slow down the rate at which we learn a new skill, that get in the way and block the process. As an instructor you work to help the automatic learning system do its job as effectively as it can. You can identify blocks to learning before you begin to instruct and as you instruct. The way you set up the training and the way that you go about instructing will either help or hinder the automatic learning system. The purpose of this book is to show you how to harness the power of the learning machine by the way you instruct. For now, do not be in any doubt about this – you must fit in with the trainee's learning machine and its method of operating. It simply is not possible for the learning machine to fit in with you.

In the next chapter I will describe the automatic learning machine in more detail to help you understand how it operates and what this means for you when you instruct. Before we do that let's make a small digression into an aspect of the learning machine that you can do something about: the learning skills we find for ourselves.

Learning skills that we find for ourselves

We have a second learning system to help us to acquire the skills we need to be human and this one is very subtle indeed. It is this: as we go through life learning new skills we remember those learning experiences and, over years of learning, we learn how to learn. We accumulate learning skills and techniques which we can use in our everyday lives to help us acquire new skills and knowings. We have to have this learning system to help us deal with our very individual experiences and lives. It is automatic in that it helps us to sort out and remember how to go about learning something new, but then we can choose whether or not we use the learning skills we have been given by it. Our learning skills form a personal toolkit which we can consciously use to help us learn what we choose to learn. Whereas our wired-in learning system is somewhat indiscriminate in what it learns, the learning skills we acquire allow us to choose to learn skills and knowledge that are important to us as individuals in the world we live in.

Because we develop our learning-skill toolkit from the learning experiences we have had in life there is great variation between our individual learning-skill toolkits. Not only does the content of each toolkit vary from individual to individual but there is great variation in the way we use the learning tools we have and when we use them. The important point for us as instructors is that the learning-skill toolkits that our trainees possess can be added to and strengthened, and we can help with this process.

Some people, perhaps many people, do not manage to gain a comprehensive toolkit of learning skills to help them learn the complex knowledge and activities that we all need to have at our fingertips. As a result of their poorly stocked learning toolboxes they experience great difficulty at school and work and often come out labelling themselves as thick or stupid. This belief, of course, makes it difficult for them to learn – it acts as a blockage. But research has shown clearly that with help to overcome the blockages we can all learn learning skills and we can strengthen the ones we already have.

It may be, then, that when an individual experiences difficulty learning the skills and knowledge necessary to live everyday life or perform his or her job, then one strategy open to you is to develop the trainee's learning skills. One well-known method of expanding the learning toolkit available to each trainee is the MUD system. Let us look at that briefly before we return to the automatic learning machine and what it means for instruction.

As we grow and learn we all begin to crystallize the experience of learning into some general rules or procedures that we can use time and time again to help us learn new things. These are the MUD skills. The learning to learn skills that we use help us to do three things: memorize, understand and do (which is where the MUD name originates).

The researchers who investigated the MUD skills discovered that the more MUD skills you have, the easier it is to learn. When the researchers examined the MUD skills of three groups of people – unemployed young people, a group beginning higher education and a group of adults starting a teaching course – they found that the first group used fewer ways of learning and used less mentally active ways than the other two groups. In addition, the unemployed young people were dependent on being taught, they were not active in their learning but waited for someone to tell them what to learn and how to learn it and then what to do with it when they had learned it. Perhaps as a result of their difficulties, they confused facts with concepts. Because they had a limited range of understanding skills (the U in MUD) they had to rely on their memorizing skills (the M in MUD) to tackle concept learning. But it does not work, and they had great difficulty learning concepts as a result. Overall, the lack of MUD learning skills had a serious outcome for the youngsters concerned.

The researchers went on from this to develop a training course intended to help people develop their full repertoire of MUD skills, and the evaluations showed that it worked. Not only did course participants use more appropriate ways of learning, they also began to take responsibility for doing their own learning instead of waiting passively for someone to teach them.

What does this mean for instructors? In practical terms, not a great deal. For most skill learning that you will come across it is the automatic learning machine you will have to deal with. The learning skills of the trainees are more geared to help them learn for themselves, although if they do have good learning skills that will help you to do your job that little bit more easily. If they have poor learning skills it will definitely hinder you and make it difficult for the trainees to gain the skills you are there to help them learn. But the good news for them is that the learning skills can be acquired, but they will not come overnight and they will need an instructor to help them acquire the skills.

Now that we have had an overview of the learning systems that you have to deal with, both automatic and acquired, let us move on to find out more about the workings of the automatic system. We will look at how skills are acquired and what that will mean for you as you plan and perform your instruction. In the next chapter I will also start to describe the basic instructional techniques and tools that you will need to help the automatic learning machine work at full effectiveness.

Bibliography

The learning machine

Dawkins, R. (1989), *The Selfish Gene*, 2nd edn, Oxford: Oxford University Press.

Leakey, R. and Lewin, R. (1992), *Origins Reconsidered: In search of what makes us human*, London: Little, Brown and Company.

Pearce, J.C. (1977), *Magical Child*, London: Paladin.

Richards, M.P.M. (ed.) (1977), *The Integration of a Child into a Social World*, Cambridge: Cambridge University Press.

Tanner, N.M. (1981), *On Becoming Human*, Cambridge: Cambridge University Press.

MUD learning skills

Downs, S. and Perry, P. (1982), 'How do I Learn?', *Journal of European Industrial Training*, 6, (6), 27–32.

Downs, S. and Perry, P. (1984), *Developing Skilled Learners, Learning to Learn in YTS*, Manpower Services Commission, R&D report no. 22, London: HMSO.

Downs, S. and Perry, P. (1984), 'Developing Learning Skills', *Journal of European Industrial Training*, 8, (1), 21–6.

Downs, S. and Perry, P. (1986), 'Can Trainers Learn to Take a Back Seat?', *Personnel Management*, March, 42–5.

Downs, S. and Perry, P. (1986), 'Skills, Strategies and Ways of Learning: Can we Help People to Learn How to Learn?', *PLET*, 22, (2), 177–80.

6

How people develop skill

Effective instructional techniques are based on how the automatic learning system works. This chapter explains how the trainee's skills develop and how you can help the trainee to develop new skills quickly.

We explained in Chapter 5 that we all have a powerful learning machine to help us learn the skills we need to get by as adults. We noted that if you can harness that automatic learning machine it will be a very powerful tool when you help the trainee to develop new skills. We also noted that if you failed to harness the learning properly it could be a very powerful hindrance to the trainee's skill development. In this chapter we consider how the learning machine works but in more detail than previously. The point is this: when you know how it works, you can start to develop instructional techniques that harness the machine's power in your favour. So, although this chapter does not deal directly with instructional technique, do not be put off. It deals with the processes that underlie instructional technique and give them their power – the trainee's learning machine.

In this chapter we describe how skills develop and what this means for you, the instructor. Later, we describe the different types of skill and their implications for how we help them to develop. I will go on to describe the stages of skill development and how you must act at each stage of the process if it is to proceed as quickly as possible. Following chapters will build on this foundation by describing the basic instructional techniques and tools that you will need to help the skills development process work at full effectiveness.

Learning and performance – two faces of skill development

Most books on training have a section that outlines people's learning processes – learning is about how information enters the head and how it is organized when it is in there. Although learning can be an important and useful, even interesting, topic to cover it is rarely of any practical use to instructors. Many psychologists who have made a study of either learning or training will tell you that learning principles are notoriously difficult to use as a way of generating training practice or instructional practice. The problem is this: for instructors, how trainees learn is not important – learning is automatic and, as we saw in the previous chapter, you cannot do much to change how the automatic learning machine operates. As instructors, we do not really need to know about learning, the learning machine takes care of that for us. What we do need to know about is how skilful actions are developed – we need to know about *performance*, not learning.

The difference between learning and performing actions can be illustrated by an analogy with a tape recorder. Learning is about how the music is picked up and stored on the tape; but we are interested in the music and how to get it to play at the right speed and volume – its performance. Learning and action are two related but separate aspects of the recording process. The rest of this book is about how to develop trainee actions that are skilled – and in this chapter we are going to talk about how skilled performance develops.

The learning machine inside our head acts as a sort of recorder. What it records (learns) and plays back (performance of actions) are the skills that we use to be ordinary human beings. Although this sounds very ordinary and humdrum, the range and complexity of skills we need to be ordinary people is vast – language skills, reasoning skills and everyday actions like reading and writing, driving, painting and playing football. Some of the skills we learn are learning skills, as we have already noted. These help us to organize information and remember it. But even these skills are installed in our heads by the learning machine's activity. So, let us now move on to find out how the learning machine plays back its recordings and what this means for instruction and instructors.

The first point that is important about the learning machine is that it can record and play back a wide range of types of skill. Different types of skill have different implications for the way in which you will set about helping someone to acquire them, so we will spend a little time looking at the different types of skill that we can develop.

Doing and thinking skills

There are many ways of dividing up the vast range of skills that people learn. For our purposes we will think about two main groups of skill. The reason that these two have been chosen is that they have differing implications for the way you must go about organizing their instruction. The first split of skills involves asking if a skill is a *doing* skill or a *thinking* skill (doing skills are also called motor skills, thinking skills are also known as cognitive skills). It does not really matter what the different skill groups are called, the point is that you can see the one happening (doing skills) but you cannot see the other happening (thinking skills). Doing skills are easy to identify – people move about and use their muscles in some way. Unless the person you are observing moves his lips as he thinks then it is not easy to tell if someone is thinking or what they are thinking about.

Now that we have a clear distinction between doing skills and cognitive skills, let us blur it a little. In reality, most doing skills involve some elements of mental activity if they are to be performed well. Think about the sewing machinist who has to sew a long, straight seam. The picking up and positioning of the fabric ready to sew involves movement, the pulling away of the fabric after sewing involves movement and the guiding of the fabric under the needle involves movement. It is clearly a doing skill but there are also elements of thinking involved – when she sews the fabric, for example, she will be watching the seam and the fabric and will be making decisions about how to pull and push the fabric as it passes under the needle so that the seam is straight. She will observe small errors, think about how to correct them as they occur and decide if the error is big enough to warrant stopping the sewing so that she can think about how to undo and correct the fault.

Open and closed skills

Doing tasks often involve some mental activity and the mental aspects of the task must be addressed by the training in addition to the more obvious movement elements of the task. Not all movement tasks demand thinking in order for them to be performed. When the skilled performer must observe and think about the world so as to adjust his or her actions to suit changing conditions then the skill is called an *open* skill – the performer must be open to the rest of the world to do the skill properly. The ones that do not require a lot of thinking can be called *closed* skills because they do not require that the trainee be open to the rest of the world as they do them. And there we have the second main type of skill category – the distinction between open and closed skills.

Closed skills are well illustrated by race swimmers. In a race swimmers will make swimming movements along the length of the swimming pool with almost no regard for what is happening around them. If they see that an opponent is swimming a little faster in the race they may increase their stroke rate or pull power to compensate, but that is all that is possible. The outside world is not important during a race – it is not necessary to match what happens to what is going on around them.

That swimming skill is very closed compared to the open swimming skills of a water polo players. Water polo players must watch what their team-mates and the opposing team are doing, must constantly adapt their actions to what is going on around them. They are watching and making many decisions about when to swim, where to swim, how to swim, when to catch and how and where to throw. They are interacting with a group of people, using their muscles and their mind. Water polo is made up of a range of skills both physical and mental and is an open skill activity.

What are the implications of the doing and thinking skills and open and closed skills for the instructor? Let us consider doing and thinking skills first and then go on to discuss open and closed skills (see Chapter 7).

Instructing doing and thinking skills

The important question for you about doing and thinking skills is whether or not there are differences in the way the two types of skill are developed. Should you do similar things or different things to help the skills develop? Recent research helps us to answer that question, especially the research concerned to understand how best to teach students to think about problems effectively. When the effective teaching strategies for mental skills are listed next to the strategies that work for movement skills, there are great similarities. In Table 6.1 I have compared the process of instruction for movement skills generally, and for a thinking skill – in this case it is how to comprehend a piece of text. The thinking skill researchers found that using the instructional techniques described in the table produced better results than either straightforward telling students how to do the comprehension task or straightforward demonstration where the instructor models their own thinking out loud for the student's benefit. Although the detailed technical content may vary between the doing and thinking skill types, effective instruction processes for both movement and thinking tasks are broadly the same.

Summary

It seems very likely that the reason that thinking and movement skills can be instructed in similar ways, even though the skills may seem very different, is due to the fact that skills are learned via the same learning machine inside the trainee's head. It is the learning machine that you are dealing with rather than the skill itself. Because the learning/performance process is the same, the instructional process will have to be similar for both movement and thinking skills. However, that is not the case for open and closed skills. These require very different instructional approaches because they are fundamentally different in their nature. Open skills have to be adapted during performance to take account of the changing environment but the closed skill performer takes little notice of what is going on around. The next chapter explains how these differences influence your instructional technique.

Table 6.1   The instruction process for doing skills compared with the process for a thinking skill

Instruction in doing, or movement skills	Instruction in thinking skills
Observe the task and identify the movements and key points to be performed – what must be done and how to do it at each stage of the task	Identify the main strategies that help with the thinking process to be developed – in this case questioning, clarifying, summarizing and predicting
Design a sequence of exercises that will help the skill(s) to develop in progressive stages	Identify a set of activities which can be used as a practice vehicle for the skills
Let the trainee see the skill being performed and emphasize what is being done and how it is done	Instructor actively models the use of the appropriate strategies, making them overt, explicit and concrete
Let the trainee practise and observe the practice – guide the trainee during performance to avoid errors and correct errors if they occur	Students model the desired activities and lead the resulting group discussion
When the trainee can perform without error allow the trainee to practise and begin to build performance to required standards	Instructor prompts, corrects and supports as necessary
When performance is to correct standards, provide lots of practice so that the skill can always be performed at that standard. Instructor begins to withdraw from the trainee, but continues to monitor what trainee is doing	Instructor monitors group activity but begins to withdraw and allow group to perform on their own

Bibliography

Allison, M.G. and Ayllon, T. (1980), 'Behavioural coaching in the development of skills in football, gymnastics and tennis', *Journal of Applied Behaviour Analysis*, **13**, (2), 297–314.

Flegg, D., Warren, A. and Law, C. (1982), *POISE: Project On Instructor Style and Effectiveness*, Cambridge: Industrial Training Research Unit Ltd.

Flegg, D. (1983), 'Developing Instructor Effectiveness – the POISE approach', *Personnel Management*, May, 38–40.

Martin, G. and Hrycaiko, D. (1983), 'Effective behavioural coaching: What's it all about?', *Journal of Sports Psychology*, **5**, (1), 8–20.

McGuinness, C. (1990), 'Talking About Thinking: The Role of Metacognition in Teaching Thinking', in Gilhooly, K.J., Keane, M.T.G., Logie, R.H. and Erdos, G. (eds), *Lines of Thinking*, Vol. 2, Chichester: John Wiley and Sons.

McGuinness, C. (1991), *Cognitive Apprenticeship: A Model of Instruction for Teaching Thinking*, paper to the British Psychological Society Annual Conference, Cognitive Section Symposium on Teaching Thinking, Bournemouth, April.

Newsham, D. and Fisher, J.M. (1972), 'What's in a style?', *Industrial and Commercial Training*, June, 291–5.

Newsham, D. (1976), *Choose an Effective Style*, research papers TR9 and TR11, Cambridge: Industrial Training Research Unit.

7

Open and closed skills

We will now start to make the instructor's job fit with the type of skill that the trainee is to develop. Open and closed skills require different instructional approaches. This chapter describes the different approaches.

It is not too difficult to teach someone to perform a closed skill; the basic instructional approach will do it every time. Typical closed skills in sport are gymnastic techniques, diving, high jump, javelin throwing, race swimming, golf swings. In all these sports the performer is either acting on objects that are not changing or the performer does not have to adjust how he or she is performing the actions to match changes in the environment. Typical closed movements in industry may be a particular sewing task or a repetitive assembly task.

Success in the use of closed skills comes from using an habitual pattern of movement that is correct for the task. The movement pattern must be performed with as little variation as possible and the performer must learn to eliminate or ignore external distractions or influences to make sure that variation is kept to a minimum. Generally, the best performer is the one who can repeat, as perfectly as possible on each repeat, the correct movement pattern.

For closed skills all we want the trainee to do is make a set of movements in a particular pattern with some reliability. The training sessions must be organized so that only the desired movements will occur. You will therefore plan ahead what movements to make, explain what must be done, show what must be done and then help the trainee to repeat the right movements often (we will develop the details of that instructional process later on). But when we want to develop a set of skills that are open in nature we run into some complexity that makes the instructional task seem more difficult.

One problem we face as instructors is that some skills are potentially both open and closed. One example is skiing. The skier skiing alone on a steady gradient will often use just one pattern of movement in a regular way – a closed skill. However, vary the slope and the curves on the slope, add two hundred other skiers and the performer has to adapt what she does to meet the changing requirements of the external world. So, the skill becomes more open than closed. Think about swimming. In a race swimming is a closed skill, but in life-saving (a much more variable and unpredictable situation) it is almost certainly an open skill. For the karate practitioner, combat with an opponent is an open skill, but the pre-arranged attack–defence patterns of kata are more closed in nature. Quite a few sports skills have this changing classification. The implication for you is that you must think carefully about the task which you are trying to teach and you must identify what aspects, if any, are open skills and what aspects are closed skill areas. They require quite different treatment – open skills must be developed in a different fashion from closed skills.

Open skills and instruction

Open skills are those that are practised in a changing world. The performer cannot rely on a steady pattern of movements to perform the task; the actions must be continually changed to meet the current situation. Some examples of this from sport are karate combat, boxing, catching or striking in almost any ball game, dodging opponents in basketball, passing in soccer, and so on. Performing in this environment using habitual, unchanging movement patterns simply will not work. The world is changing and the movements and their timing pattern will have to vary with the demands of the situation.

These open skill tasks must be developed in a training environment where change is the rule. Instead of practising the same movement over and over again, it is more useful to practise the movement as and when it is called for and in the best pattern for the changing environment. But there is a problem. If the training environment is too changeable then the practice is basically learning on the job and is little different to having no instruction at all. So the practice environment must be carefully designed to allow useful practice in some aspects of the skill rather than all aspects of the skill. As the chosen aspects are mastered, new environments or practice conditions must be introduced that help to develop new patterns of skill while also continuing with practice of the established patterns.

Changing practice conditions and open skills demand that the performer be adaptable, flexible in response, able to read the situation, able to anticipate what will happen next. So the practice conditions you design must also be designed to allow the trainee to practise being adaptable, flexible in response, able to read the situation, able to anticipate what will happen next.

But that is not all. You must also be there to help those skills develop. You will be actively explaining what to do and how to do it. You will be telling the performer what to look for in the situation, how to tell when an opponent is about to do a particular action, and so on. The trainee needs help to use the information which the external world is presenting to them as they practise their open skills. What patterns of rebound occur for balls travelling in a particular direction? What can an opponent do and not do when standing in a particular position? What is your opponent's favourite play and how can you predict it and counter it? All these issues must be addressed by you, the instructor, and you must help the trainee prepare for the changes that will occur as they practise the open skill. You must then help them to see when they are coming and react accordingly. When that is happening, your trainee will be developing the right skills.

So, instructing open skills demands that you design practice conditions that will allow the skill to develop and that you are present to guide the trainee as they perform.

Closed skills and instruction

In contrast, closed skill practice must allow the performance of a fixed, unchanging pattern of movement. Any variation in that one fixed pattern will destroy what you are trying to achieve. Imagine trying to teach a gymnast to perform a forward somersault on the beam if the beam wobbled and tipped every time they tried to perform the manoeuvre. Compare the success likely if the beam was rock solid and did not move.

Varying the instructional approach as necessary

Although it is fairly easy to see how you can help the trainee in closed skill practice, it is less easy to see how to help in the changing environment of an open skill. Make no mistake about it – you and your instruction are important, if not vital, factors in the rapid and efficient development of both closed and open skills. You will be doing similar instructional things in both skill types but the details of your approach will vary.

In both open and closed skill types you will identify, in advance, what the key points of the skill to be learned are. For closed skills that may be the correct pattern of movement, for open skills that may be information that helps the trainee to recognize what to do next and when to do it.

Both open and closed skill types demand carefully planned practice. Asking someone to perform a complex open skill too soon will swamp them. Instead of learning they will barely be able to cope. The aim of structured practice is that the trainee develops a few simple skills or parts of a skill in a realistic environment that does not swamp them with too much information and challenge. One of the main reasons why trainees fail is that they are being asked to do too many new things at once. Ask yourself this: when you were learning to drive, could you drive through rush-hour traffic, navigate and hold a conversation with your driving instructor – all at the same time and on your second lesson too? Of course not. That is why you will have to structure the practice sessions so carefully. Training exercises and skill practice have to set achievable targets of performance and have to allow skill development. If it is too demanding the trainee will not be able to do what is asked.

Effective instruction in both open and closed skill types includes you being present to tell the trainee how they are doing. The trainee will be too busy to be able to understand how well they are doing or they will be too ignorant to know – they are trainees after all. Successful and effective instructors tell the trainees how well they are doing, but there is a technique for doing this effectively and a range of techniques for doing it badly. How to do it effectively is explained in Chapters 13 and 14.

Finally, both open and closed skill types demand that you observe what is happening to the trainee and correct mistakes. This has to be done immediately in the early stages of skill development. Such is the power of the learning machine that mistakes which are repeated even a few times will become permanent patterns of behaviour. Once they are learned in this way they cannot be unlearned. One reason why the trainees of poor instructors take longer to develop than the trainees of good instructors is that the poor instructors allow their trainees to practise various methods. The trainees are therefore trying to learn a thousand methods instead of just one – the right one. Because of the variation the trainee cannot tell when he or she makes a mistake in performance because every performance feels different. The trainee who practises just one method will always be able to tell when the method has changed – it will feel different in some way.

There is an old adage – practice makes perfect. It doesn't. Practice makes permanent. If the method is wrong, or if the trainee does something at the wrong time, practice alone will not change it. Practising the wrong method merely produces an increased ability to do it wrong next time. Only effective instruction will consistently produce the correct method and the right timing of actions. When those elements are right, further practice will make them permanent. That is true for both open and closed skills.

The hierarchy of skills that make up open skills

We have already noted in the previous chapter that for some tasks the boundary between open and closed skills is flexible. Generally, this is true for any open skill. Open skills are made up of combinations of closed skills, plus other skills specific to the open skill itself. That probably needs some explanation, so here it is.

What I am talking about here is important if we are to instruct effectively. The idea is called the hierarchy of skill and its main function for you is to help you to decide how best to structure the training practice sessions. The basics behind the hierarchy of skill is simple: open skills are made up of a range of closed skills which are then grouped into actions that can be performed as needed. These combinations are fitted on to specific events happening in the external world – and that forms the open part of the skilled task overall. Figures 7.1–7.3 explain how the hierarchy works.

First the performer has to learn the appropriate closed skills that will be used to perform the open skill task (Figure 7.1). These are developed one at a time, generally, but as several are mastered it often happens that they are practised in combination. So the next level of the open skill to be learned is the combination basic skills (Figure 7.2). Combinations of basic skill can of course still remain closed in nature. But the next level in the skill hierarchy is where the open skill proper begins to develop. Open skills rely heavily on decision making – decisions about opponents' intentions, directions of ball rebound, team member availability, and so on. When the environment has been read in this way, the performer then decides what basic or combination movements to use (Figure 7.3).

The key skill at the open level is about reading the situation and choosing what to do. That choice is, of course, limited to what has been learnt already – in other words the performer can select what to do only from what is

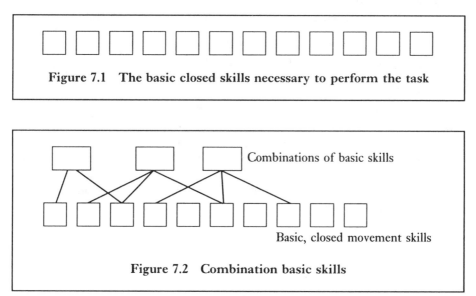

Figure 7.1   The basic closed skills necessary to perform the task

Combinations of basic skills

Basic, closed movement skills

Figure 7.2   Combination basic skills

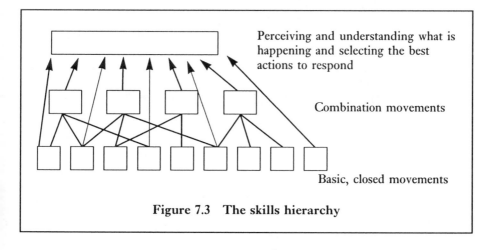

Perceiving and understanding what is happening and selecting the best actions to respond

Combination movements

Basic, closed movements

Figure 7.3   The skills hierarchy

available in his head. So the effectiveness of the decision is partly dependent on the skill base the performer is drawing on. But the decision making is also dependent on how well the performer can perceive and understand what is happening in the outside world. That is a skill in itself and it must be practised at this stage of open skill development.

Summary

That then is the skill hierarchy. Each level of the hierarchy and each skill within it requires a similar instructional approach but a differing practice situation to develop the different skills that are present at each level. The basic skills will be developed using a closed skill approach, the combination skills will be developed by using both a closed skill approach and an open skill approach to practice. The decision skill level will be developed by using an open skill practice schedule. However, within the differing practice schedules, a very similar instructional approach will be used. That approach is explained in later chapters.

A very skilled performer of an open skill is able to make decisions very quickly. The decisions must also be consistently accurate. In many tasks of a closed nature something similar is also often necessary. The closed skill task must be performed quickly, with speed, and performed accurately and reliably on each occasion. In fact most skills must be performed at speed and also with reliable accuracy. We therefore need to think about how to develop speed and accuracy of performance, and the next chapter addresses this problem.

Bibliography

Cratty, B.J. (1973), *Movement Behaviour and Motor Learning*, 3rd edn, Philadelphia: Lea and Febiger.

Holding, D.H. (1965), *Principles of Training*, Oxford: Pergamon Press.

Holding, D.H. (ed.) (1989), *Human Skills*, 2nd edn, Chichester: John Wiley and Sons.

Robb, M.D. (1972), *The Dynamics of Motor-Skill Acquisition*, Englewood Cliffs, NJ: Prentice Hall.

Schmidt, R.A. (1975), *Motor Skills*, London: Harper and Row.

8

Developing speed and accuracy of movement

Many skills must be performed with both speed and accuracy, but which should be developed first? Is it enough to concentrate on accuracy in instruction and trust that speed will come? This chapter examines the research evidence and outlines appropriate instructing strategies.

Many tasks must be performed accurately and with speed. This is true in both sport and industry. For example: a boxer with a technically perfect punch is not a winner if that punch is so slow that the opponent can avoid it. Karate provides a better sporting example perhaps, because there are a wide range of kicks, blocks and attacks. The films with martial arts fighters as stars demonstrate the sort of speed necessary and the range of techniques that are used at speed. But speed alone is not enough. The fighters must also use an accurate technique. We are all familiar with the martial arts masters who are able to break several one-inch boards with one fast blow or kick. Imagine trying to break a brick with a high-speed blow of the hand but with the hand held incorrectly – result, broken bones!

Many industrial tasks demand speed of action as well as accuracy of action. For example, a sewing machinist in a factory manufacturing shirts will often perform just one sewing operation on the garment (say, attaching a breast pocket to a shirt) and then pass it on to the next machinist carrying out the next operation in the assembly process. Any inaccuracy in the sewing will result in wobbly stitching or sewing that runs off the edge of the pocket and the machinist will be penalized for poor-quality work. In addition the machinist's colleagues may have difficulty performing their task because the sewing has not been completed properly. If the machinist slows down to increase accuracy, however, other workers will have to work at his or her speed, and as he or she is paid on piece-work he or she will earn low wages, and so will his or her colleagues. In addition, the slow speed across the production floor will cause factory output to fall and could, in the long term, threaten everyone's employment. So, for the sewing machinist, as for many other assembly workers, speed and accuracy are both very important aspects of the job they perform.

How do speed and accuracy develop? Anyone who has tried to perform an unfamiliar task quickly and accurately will know that speed and accuracy are not easy to acquire. Game shows often depend on this problem in the games they design for their contestants. Speed up and mistakes abound, slow down and the other team may ice more cakes or stuff more cuddly toys. The audience has a wonderful entertainment at the expense of the contestants struggling with the problem of how to be both accurate and fast at the unfamiliar task.

At the beginning of learning a new task, therefore, we can expect our trainee to experience difficulties similar to those of the game show contestants. What happens later on? Do speed and accuracy arrive together in some mysterious fashion, or do they have to be worked at? And if they have to be worked at, how should one go about it? Do we need instructors to help, or can we do it on our own? Let us answer these questions by looking at research in sport and industry. First we will look at how the speed of a task develops.

A much-quoted study in training circles some years ago was Crossman's investigation of cigar makers learning to make cigars using purpose-built machines. That investigation was carried out in the 1950s when cigar makers were, perhaps, more common than they are now. The study was simple. Crossman began to keep records of the number of cigars produced by a sample of new recruits and monitored their cigar production over a two-year period. In this period they produced about three million cigars and over the whole of this period they continued to increase the speed at which they produced them. At first the increases in speed were large, later the increases in speed were less marked and became less and less so as the period of time increased. After about two years the cigar makers reached the maximum speed they could achieve and no more increase was observed. Crossman notes in his article that other studies exploring other tasks in other industries also found that speed increases over a period of time working on the job and then reaches a level at which no more improvement appears possible.

There have been similar findings in sport-based research. Studies of karate practitioners have found that the speed of both simple punches (where the feet do not move) and moving punches (where a step forward is taken as the punch is executed) increased over many years of practice. By filming practitioners as they performed the techniques it was possible to measure the speed of the techniques following different periods of time practising karate. It was found that a karate practitioner of a few months was twice as slow as one who had practised karate for about five years; that is, as with cigar rolling, the speed at which the actions can be performed increases with increasing length of practice.

But that is not all. The karate studies also showed that the speed of parts of the punch changed in different ways as the practice period increased. Karate practitioners with about ten years' experience were, overall, only a little faster than those with five years' experience but some parts of their punch technique were much faster. They had changed the way they performed the punching action with increased practice.

This change of method over time is a common finding with many movement tasks. As skill develops it seems that speed increases primarily by the development of better, more efficient patterns of movement rather than by faster movements alone. Let us think about that further.

Crossman's investigation was really concerned with trying to understand how speed of action increases. His investigation was one of several tackling the same problem. The theory that he put forward is this: the trainee starts off trying to do a task with a particular pattern of movements which, in the absence of instruction, is chosen at random. Because some movements are longer or more complicated than others there is a limit to the speed at which that pattern of movement can be performed. Beyond that speed, the movements themselves get in the way. Thus the trainee, in an attempt to speed up task performance, changes the pattern of movements to try to find one which will produce the same task outcome but which can be performed faster. This is easier in the early stages of training than it is in the later stages of training when fairly efficient patterns have been discovered. Speed gain therefore can be expected to be faster in the early stages than in the later stages of practice (not forgetting that in the very early stages of practice movement itself will tend to be slow anyway). As the methods used become more refined the time to perform the task (task speed) decreases. Eventually there is a pattern of movement that cannot be bettered and the speed at which this can be performed can be pushed to the limit. At this point, overall speed gain ceases – for the cigar makers this process took two years and about three million cigars; the karate practitioners took longer.

This would be fine if every trainee were to vary the methods used and find the fastest ones with equal ease. Other investigators have found that this does not happen. Careful studies of trainees given the freedom to choose the method of performing a task found that they chose methods at random. When the chosen method was well established it was not always changed, but when it was changed the trainees changed it at random again. Hence, even if the trainee tried to change a slow method to a faster one there was a good chance that the new method would be slower, or at least no faster, than the one they started with.

Allowing trainees to choose their own methods and adapt those methods is a lottery. Most will not find a faster method of working and so will not speed up. Some of the practical implications of this for individuals can be gauged from what happened on an instructor training course some years ago.

Some years ago a clothing manufacturer ran a training course for its instructors. As the course ran at the factory premises there was a good opportunity to have the instructors practise their instructional technique on 'real live' trainees. On the last day of the programme the tutor arranged for some of the young sewing trainees to be used as training guinea pigs. One of the instructors was allocated Allison for the day. The instructor's task was to teach Allison a sewing job that was fairly difficult because it required both speed and accuracy to perform correctly. The earlier parts of the instructor course had allowed the instructor to prepare all the training exercises and resources that were necessary. By the end of the day Allison had achieved a speed half that required to perform the job on the factory floor and was able to sew with the accuracy necessary to meet the factory's quality inspection standards. This sort of training result usually required several weeks to achieve under the factory's usual training system but here it had been achieved in one day. Surprisingly the instructors on the course were not as pleased as might be expected. They knew that Allison was due to be sacked that very day. The reason was that she had failed to increase her speed on the sewing tasks she had been given in the factory. As a result of their instructor training, they also knew why Allison had made no progress: she had been allowed to choose her own sewing methods over the six weeks she had been employed. As she varied her sewing method her sewing quality varied but her sewing speed did not increase. Without proper advice on how to vary methods to increase speed she had to rely on random changes in method and, in her case, these had not increased speed. Because of her lack of progress she was out of a job at the age of 16 in an area of high unemployment. The instructors, however, had just proved that she could be trained by using effective instructional techniques. No wonder they were upset!

Typing provides another example of how methods of work and speed of work are related and the effect they can have on each other. Typing is very easy. It is quite possible for a complete beginner to type a letter after a few minutes. However, as we all know, the letter will be typed with two fingers and it will take a long time to produce. With more practice it is possible to type a letter with two fingers in a fairly short time. But using two fingers is inherently slow. There will come a time when it just is not possible to type any faster with two fingers. If you want to type faster you will have to use more fingers, so you change method and begin to use other fingers. At the start you will have to slow down and take care, but after a while speed will increase and you probably will be typing a little faster than you could with two fingers. You can go on with this process, bringing more and more fingers into play, getting faster and faster until eventually the limiting factor on the speed you can type at will be how often you have to look at the words you want to type and how fast you can find the letters on the keyboard. If you want to go yet faster you will have to learn how to touch-type, using all your fingers without looking at the type-writer keys. So, it is back to very slow typing for a while until you develop the touch-type technique.

There are several lessons to be learned from thinking about typing. First, however much you want to go fast, the method you use may prevent you gaining the speed you want. Second, if you use the right method from the start you will gain speed and accuracy much more quickly than if you have to change your methods in the hope of speeding up. You will not have to go through the process of learning one method to a slow speed, learning a second method to a faster speed, learning a third method to faster speed still, and so on. It would make sense to learn the right method right from the start, wouldn't it? The third lesson, then, is that it would be very useful to have someone show you the right method, right from the start. That is a job that an instructor can do.

Studies of training in the 1940s found that when workers were given an efficient method of working they developed speed faster than those trainees left to develop their own methods of working. The studies also found that established workers who had been left to train themselves used methods of working that were very inefficient and slow. When they were shown efficient methods of working their speed, and more interestingly their accuracy, improved.

It should be clear now that the way in which a job is done will influence the speed that can be achieved. There are many industrial tasks which demand both high speed and high accuracy. Many people have had to learn these tasks to earn their living. We might expect, then, that there would be some distilled wisdom that would say how to go about teaching someone to be both very fast and very accurate. What is the usual advice for developing speed and accuracy? It is simple – most trainees are told that they should take their time and make sure they get it right and that speed will come with practice. Does that sound reasonable advice? Luckily, there has been a fair amount of research investigating this problem. Most investigations into speed and accuracy of method have been carried out in sport, a few have been carried out in industry. First, let us see what the sports studies tell us.

Speed versus accuracy emphasis in sport tasks instruction

Most research effort has been directed at understanding how to increase accuracy rather than speed. Generally, the investigations follow a similar pattern: several groups are formed and each group is given different instructions about how to carry out a task. The groups all have the same task to perform but one is told to be as accurate as possible, another is told to be as fast as possible, a third is told to be both fast and accurate and a fourth group may be given no instructions at all. The groups are all allowed to perform the task and the speed and accuracy of each group is measured.

When the task to be learned was a forehand tennis stroke it was found that the group which had gone for speed could then transfer the speed emphasis they had learned to an accuracy emphasis and could then be both fast and accurate, but a group which had learned to be accurate could not then become fast. In tennis strokes, then, the speed must be learned before accuracy.

In golf, the group that were told to be accurate were found to slow down the speed of their swing. As with tennis strokes, when speed groups were asked to become accurate they could transfer the speed they had learned and became both faster and more accurate.

A third sports study investigated the effect of speed and accuracy instructions on a striking movement – a punch or slap. The findings agreed with the others: where speed was an important part of the task it should be taught from the start of training. If accuracy is also important, then both speed and accuracy should be emphasized from the start of training. So much for sporting tasks. What about industrial tasks?

Speed versus accuracy emphasis in industrial tasks instruction

Although there have not been many studies in industry (studies of sewing are one area) the results are the same as for sport. First the trainee must be given an efficient method of work to perform, then the speed at which the task is carried out is emphasized and the accuracy of the method controlled.

We might also recall the cigar rollers and the karate practitioners discussed above in detail. In both examples there is a continual encouragement to be fast: karate's driving emphasis on speed comes from the need to strike one's opponent before he hits you. In the case of the cigar makers, they were driven by production pressures and the speed of the machine they operated. In both cases the pressure continued to develop speed over many years.

Instructing to develop speed and accuracy

The research findings are very clear. The old adage 'get it right and speed will come' is wrong. When speed and accuracy are important to the correct performance of the task then at the start of training speed should be given a greater emphasis, on balance, than accuracy. As training progresses both should be emphasized.

Why is this true? Training recommendations which are found to work are very useful. But a theme through this book is that what the instructor does is driven by the internal skill learning processes of the trainee. So what is happening in the trainee's head to make speed more important than the accuracy of methods of work?

We have to ask what is learned when someone develops an action skill. First, the most obvious thing is the movements that make up the action. But there is also something subtle. Any dancer will know that there is a rhythm involved in any dance. Any pattern of movement has a rhythm – walking and running have very clear rhythms but there are some tempos which are perhaps too slow to be noticed. Nevertheless every pattern of movement has a timing aspect to it. When we learn a set of actions it is very like making a tape recording of the movements. If we think of a tape recording then we can think of the particular movements and actions as like the music being recorded. They are very variable, perhaps infinitely variable in nature, and they can be fast or slow. But underlying the recording is the speed at which we run the tape past the recording heads. We can run it fast or slow, but we must play it back at exactly the same speed or we will never be able to appreciate the music because it will be distorted.

When we learn a pattern of movements we also learn the speed that we must play those movements back. If we learn a slow speed or rhythm of movement then we will play back those movements at a slow speed. When developing skills which require speed, therefore, we must help the trainee to learn the skills at the right speed, right from the start of training.

Summary

Speed and accuracy are two sides of the same skill coin. Although there is a strong and widespread belief in industry that the instructor should focus on developing accuracy because speed will follow, that is not true. The research is clear: if you want speed and accuracy, you must train for both and preferably right from the start of training. However, it is important to remember that speed comes primarily from the use of an efficient movement pattern. It is vital that the method the trainee uses is a method which will allow the required accuracy and speed. When speed is slow in developing, you should look to the method that is used. There is a good chance that it is the method being used that is preventing the speed from developing.

Bibliography

Fitts, P.M. (1966), 'Cognitive aspects of information processing: III. set for speed and accuracy', *Journal of Experimental Psychology*, 71, 849–57.

Gershoni, H. (1979), 'An investigation of behaviour changes of subjects learning manual tasks', *Ergonomics*, 22, (11), 1195–1206.

Jordan, W.L. (1965), *The Results of Speed and Accuracy Emphases on the Learning of a Selected Motor Skill in Golf*, unpublished doctoral dissertation, University of Minnesota.

Ladhams, G.H. (1952), 'A New Method For Training Operators', *Personnel*, 28, 471–7.

Lindahl, L.G. (1945), 'Movement Analysis as an Industrial Training Method', *Journal of Applied Psychology*, 29, 420–36.

Pearcey, A.R.H. (1976), 'A Brief Description of Improved Machinist Training', *Bobbin*, September, 62 ff.

Robb, M.D. (1972), *The Dynamics of Motor-Skill Acquisition*, Englewood Cliffs, NJ: Prentice Hall.

Solley, W.H. (1951), 'Speed, Accuracy, and Speed and Accuracy as an Initial Directive in Motor Learning', *Motor Skills Research Exchange*, 3, 76–7.

Woods, J.B. (1964), *The Effect of Varied Instructional Emphasis on the Development of a Motor Skill*, unpublished doctoral dissertation, University of Minnesota.

9

The three stages of skill development

In earlier chapters I explained how the instructor's approach had to vary according to the type of skill to be developed. The instructional approach also varies depending on whether speed or accuracy is to be developed. The instructor must also change technique as the trainee's skill develops to take account of the differing requirements of the trainee at each stage of skill development. This chapter explains what must be done and when.

The previous chapter finished on a high note: 'When developing skills that require speed we must help the trainee to learn the skills at the right speed, right from the start of training.' There is a bit of a difficulty with this, though, and it will require tremendous instructional skill to overcome that difficulty. In fact, this difficulty is the key to understanding why instructors have to do what they have to do. It will not take long to explain.

Whatever skill we develop has to go through the same stages of development. The stages were first described by a group of instructors taking part in a research study in the early 1960s. The researcher concerned asked them how skills developed and found the instructors had noticed three main stages in the skill development of their trainees:

1. a stage where the trainee attempted to understand the task;
2. a stage where the trainee tried to do the task, but had to concentrate hard;
3. a stage where the task performance became automatic and the trainee did not have to concentrate to perform it.

Although the stages have been given different names by different writers since then, the three stages crop up again and again in the research literature on skill development. Each stage has particular implications for you as you try to instruct. Other research has found that you must do certain things in each stage if the skill is to develop as rapidly as possible. If you do something else that is not appropriate for that skill stage you may well disrupt the automatic process of skill development. So let us turn to a description of the three stages and the implications of each for instruction.

Stage 1. Understanding the task

The first stage in trying to learn a task is to try to understand what must be done. That is true whether the task is a movement task or a mental task. When there is no instructor to help a trainee will often try to think through the task and plan out what to do and in what sequence to do it. They will try to build a mental picture of themselves performing the task. They may be able to watch someone else performing the task and try to copy what they see. Of course there is a problem with this. Because the task is new to the trainee, they will not know what to watch out for as the task is performed. They will see someone performing the task but may spend all their time watching wrong aspects of the task. They may miss the important tricks of the trade that help the skilled performer do the job. New recruits about to be trained as sewing machinists often watch the sewing machine and the speed of the needle – industrial sewing machines operate at a much faster speed than domestic machines. The trainees are new to the factory and they look about them at all the bustle and activity. What they do not watch are the hands of the sewing machinist doing the demonstration. They do not notice the way that the machinist has laid out the fabric around the sewing machine so that it is easy to pick up and position. They do not notice the way in which he or she holds the fabric in a very specific way to help it travel under the needle. Because no one is there to tell them, they will be unaware of the sewing faults that cause the skilled machinist to stop and unpick the work.

When instructors are present they will often arrange for a demonstration of someone performing the task in a skilled fashion. Sometimes an instructor will perform the task and ask the trainees to watch carefully. Of course, if the trainees have not been told what to watch for they may as well have no instructor present – they will be guessing. You must make sure, therefore, that the trainees watch the demonstration and understand what is being done and how it is being done. They must be told what to look at, and they must be helped to see what is happening that is important. At the end of the demonstration they must understand what they have just seen. A demonstration is only as good as the explanation that accompanies it.

During this stage of developing a skill the trainee will try to work out the task cues that will tell them what to do next. They will watch out for events that occur as the task proceeds and they will observe responses that are made. As they gain proficiency at performing the task much of what they pay attention to now will be ignored. That is mostly because everything gained at this stage becomes automatic later on and does not need to be noticed. So, although this stage is useful it is not necessarily as important as many instructors and training books suggest. Many books about instruction emphasize the importance of good demonstration in instruction. Many training courses for instructors help them to plan out and rehearse demonstrations to groups of trainees. But the point about demonstration is that it must aid understanding. If the instructor is busy doing a wonderful demonstration and the trainees are not paying attention, then the demonstration is wonderful but ineffective.

There is another relevant point here. Practical experience and research evidence show that demonstrations do not really help trainees to do a task. True, a good demonstration that expands the trainee's understanding is useful; but there is much more to the development of skill and those other aspects of instruction must be attended to as well. In fact, they are more important than demonstration. Why?

We have two separate systems in our brain which deal with different aspects of the world. One system is concerned with words and the understandings and knowledge that words open up to us – let's call it the word brain. The other system works everything else. The word system is where our I, or our consciousness, lives. We think in terms of words, we talk to ourselves and to each other using words. We express our emotions in words. Therefore we tend to think that we are made up of the words we use.

The other system, lacking words, tends to be ignored by us living in the word brain. We take it for granted that we can walk, we seldom wish to explain to others what it feels like to walk, breathe or move about. This system is the one we have had for millions of years and as a result it does its job very well indeed. Let us call this brain system the body brain.

The ability to talk and think in terms of words is relatively new in an evolutionary sense. Because of this fact the two brains do not talk to each other very easily; they speak, as it were, in different languages. The word brain expresses itself using words, the body brain expresses itself using movement. What does this mean for skill development?

First, let us think about movement-based skills such as tennis or golf or karate. A demonstration based on words will prepare the word brain for action but it is the body brain that must learn the skill, so the demonstration will not help a great deal. The word brain cannot easily explain to the body brain what must be done and, when it tries to, it continually interferes with the body brain's performance of the task. If we are to learn the movement skill we must help the body brain to develop its expertise and we must turn off the word brain and its continual attempts to try to control what is happening. If we can manage to do that then the body brain's millions of years of experience will quickly gain proficiency at the task. One sports coach, Tim Gallwey (see the bibliography at the end of this chapter), has developed a system of coaching based on shutting down the word brain so the body brain can get on with the job of developing skill. We will talk about what you can do to help this process when we discuss stage 2 of skill development.

If the task to be performed is mostly knowledge-based (say, a task where procedures are important) with little movement – for example, piloting an aircraft – then a word-based demonstration becomes more useful. That is because the task is largely based within the word brain's domain of words and knowledge. For example, one flying instructor would carry out detailed discussion of the flight manoeuvres to be performed. This discussion would list and explain the exact sensory clues that were important at each stage of the manoeuvre to be performed and the exact sequence of responses that had to be made by the trainee to each of the sensory cues. He interspersed each of these in-depth discussions with demonstration flights which were then followed by further discussion. This process reduced the average time for a novice to be ready for solo flight from ten hours to under four hours.

In this first stage of learning a skill the trainee must gain some understanding of the task to be performed: they must have some idea of what they are to do. Demonstration is a useful way of helping the trainee to gain this understanding. A poor demonstration will not develop understanding but a good one will. Even a good demonstration, however, has a limited use for many tasks, particularly those that are primarily movement tasks. For these tasks it is more important that the trainee starts to perform the task because that is when learning and skill development will begin to occur: as the body brain swings into action. When a task is more knowledge-based – and hence a word brain task – then a detailed discussion that describes the necessary knowledge can be supplemented by demonstration. With these tasks, the discussion and the demonstration are important precursors to skilled performance. For both types of tasks, though, it is important to be aware that these techniques are useful only at the start of training. As skill develops demonstration loses its instructional value and other instructional techniques become important. Let us talk about those now as we consider the second stage of skill development.

Stage 2. Trying to do the task

The second stage of skill development is when the trainee attempts to perform the task. This is when skill development proper begins. In reality, this stage tends to blur with stage 1; the trainee's understanding is often poor when they try the task for the first time. Performing the task helps to enrich understanding. So it is a little artificial to try and be strict about when stage 1 finishes and stage 2 begins. If stage 1 is characterized by demonstrations and discussions, then stage 2 is characterized by the trainee attempting to perform the task and making many mistakes in the process. Stage 2 is the incompetent, clumsy, 'klutz' stage of skill development. By the end of this stage the trainee has eliminated errors in performance and has probably achieved or come close to achieving the performance standards required.

For the trainee, stage 2 is very important. In this stage the task is mastered, although there is the opportunity for many errors in the process of gaining mastery; and it is in this stage that you make the most significant contributions to the process of skill development – significant both in terms of the amount of contribution and of the quality of contribution. Let us now turn to what you do to help skill develop in stage 2.

We have seen earlier that the trainee's practice needs to be carefully structured and organized. When practice is properly designed the right skills will be developed and the nature of the practice will help the skills to develop.

It is in stage 2 of skill development that skill practice begins. Therefore the first way that you help skill develop in stage 2 is to organize and plan the practice routine that is to be followed. For simple movement tasks, the practice may be a sequence of practice exercises with carefully predetermined movements that must be performed at a specific speed and with a specific accuracy before they can be said to be mastered. For more open skills involving reading a situation and responding appropriately, the practice may involve carefully structured simulations of the real-life task. Some simulations may be simple, such as a predetermined sparring sequence (in a combat skill) or a role-play situation (in a communication-based skill). Other simulations may be more complex and require very detailed computer-controlled equipment – for example, a flight simulator or a simulation of a nuclear power station control room. Whatever the detail of the simulation, the aim is to present a realistic situation that will help the trainee to spot important clues and associate the right responses to those clues. In many cases it is important for you to be on hand to offer advice and guidance so as to help the trainee avoid error and practise the correct method – and that is the second way that you can help in this second stage of skill development.

The second stage is when the trainee begins to try the task for the first time. Because everything is new to the trainee the task will be performed at first in a somewhat haphazard fashion: the internal rules that the trainee will use later on to guide his or her movements and decisions do not exist yet. The whole point of the early activity is to lay down in the body brain's memory the rules that will be used to generate the skilled actions later on. The process is usually known as trial and error. However, if an instructor is there who knows what should be done and how it should be done there is less error and hence a better-quality series of trials. There are two important prerequisites before this help can be given:

1. You must know the task in detail so that the best advice can be given. This does not mean that you can do the task to full performance. It is a common myth (in industry at least) that an ideal instructor is someone who is a high performer on the task. While it can be very useful to have an insider's view of how a task is best performed, there is no real need for the instructor to be able to perform the task as well as the trainee. As a general rule, the best instructor is one who understands a task and is able to help another to perform it. Being an expert at performing it themselves is useful, but in itself is not an adequate qualification for instruction. Careful pre-preparation using the right instructional techniques (discussed in following chapters) will help you to know what to look for and what advice to offer the trainee as they try to perform the task.

2. You must have time available to be with the trainee. The process of error correction and helping the trainee avoid error is time-consuming. It is not a case of popping over every now and then. To be most effective you must be continuously present, and working with the trainee, in the very early part of stage 2. As errors are avoided with your help, the trainee quickly

learns to do the task correctly. There will be progressively more opportunity for you to be absent as the trainee's performance improves. But even
then you should not be away for long and if safety is a factor in the task it
is even more important for you to be present. Research studies have found
that when you have to split your attention between several trainees the
average time needed for the trainees to achieve the desired performance
increases dramatically for each additional trainee involved. When you can
deal with one trainee at a time the skills develop very quickly indeed.

Now that we have an instructor who knows the task to be developed and has
the time to instruct, what is involved in helping the trainee master the task in
stage 2? You will do two things:

1. First, observe what the trainee is doing and prompt the trainee when
   important parts of the task are about to happen. It might be that in the
   demonstrations and discussions before the practice you described a particular response that the trainee must make to a particular event. As the
   trainee performs the task you will watch and will warn the trainee when
   the particular event is about to happen. That will serve two purposes: it
   will warn the trainee to be prepared to make the response and it will give
   the trainee an opportunity to see the event and remember it. The next time
   that the event occurs the trainee is doubly prepared as a result. They will
   be more likely to be able to see the event and they will be more able to
   respond appropriately. It is very likely that several attempts will be needed
   before the trainee does not need prompts. This is discussed in more detail
   in Chapter 14.
2. When the trainee makes the response there are two possibilities. First, the
   response was incorrect in some way or, second, the response was correct. If
   an incorrect response was made, you will have to explain what was wrong
   and how to do it right. It is not enough to call out 'That was wrong!', the
   trainee needs to know what to do and when to do it. The explanation is the
   important part. It is important that the explanation and correction come as
   soon as possible after the mistake. The aim is to put the mistake right
   before it is repeated. This is discussed in more detail in Chapter 15. If the
   trainee makes the right response at the right time, then it is important to
   tell the trainee. In the early stages of struggling to perform a new task,
   trainees are concentrating and cannot necessarily notice that they have done
   something well. Because the task is new to them they may not be able to
   recognize they have done it well. By telling them immediately you are
   giving them the chance to remember how it felt to do it the correct way.
   That will increase the possibility of their doing it correctly the next time.

In the early parts of the second stage of skill development the trainee will make
many mistakes. These cannot be avoided as that is the way that skills develop.
You can reduce the number of mistakes and increase the chance of correct
performance, however, by prompting as the trainee performs, correcting when

the trainee does it wrong and telling the trainee when the task is being performed correctly. Obviously, as this process occurs, the trainee is very likely to perform the task properly each time. That means that the automatic learning machine records only the right parts of the skill and, as a result, skill develops very quickly. Because the trainee only ever performs the right methods it becomes very easy for him or her to notice if things are going wrong and correct them as the task is performed. If the trainee is not corrected and does not get guidance every repetition of the task will be different and it becomes impossible for the trainee to notice method variation and correct it. With good instruction in the second stage of skill development the trainee quickly achieves the required performance standards on the task being practised – and that is when stage 3 of skill development begins to happen.

Stage 3. The task performance becomes automatic

As soon as the trainee begins to perform the task in the required fashion it is important that practice is continued. In the final stage of skill development the task is performed many times so that the correct performance is burned into the memory. In this stage of skill development the performance of the task ceases to be something to think about and becomes something that is automatic, requiring no mental effort to perform. Indeed, one of the distinguishing symptoms of a very skilled performer is that their performance seems effortless, they appear to have all the time in the world to do the task, they have time to think as they perform. These are all indications that the task's performance has become so automatic it is almost like a reflex action. Getting to this end state is not a short journey. It needs a lot of practice to achieve this level of skill.

The second stage of skill development moves the trainee from the point of making mistakes to performance to the desired criteria. As soon as the trainee can perform the task to the required standards, they are in the third stage of skill development. If practice stops at that point the performance that is recorded by the learning machine will be an average of all the previous performances and because these were less than perfect the subsequent performance will be, on the whole, less than perfect. If a perfect performance is desired, it will be necessary to practise the perfect performance many times until the average that the learning machine records is a perfect average – the more perfect performances the trainee produces the more likely it is that the average is perfect. So, in the third stage of skill development, you must arrange for the trainee to practise the task again and again. It is only with this repetition that the task's performance becomes automatic and completely skilful.

I noted earlier that practice does not make perfect – only effective instruction makes perfect. Practice makes permanent, and a permanent record of the skill is what develops in the third stage of skill development.

Summary

The trainee's skill development goes through a series of stages. At each stage you must act differently if the skill is to develop quickly. In the first stage of skill development the trainee is both ignorant of what to do and incompetent in performance. You must help the trainee to gain an understanding of what is to be done and how it is to be done. This will not develop skilled performance on its own, however. For that the trainee must move to the second stage where they attempt to do the task for the first time. There will be many mistakes made initially in this stage. You must guide and correct the trainee's performance until they can achieve the necessary speed and accuracy on the task. When that occurs the trainee is performing the task properly for the first time. That is the beginning of the third stage of skill development. Here, you will arrange practice conditions which allow and encourage the correct performance of the skill. That repetition will help the skill to become a permanent record in the trainee's head. At that point, the trainee is fully skilled.

Overview: skills and instruction

Let us put all of the information about the learning machine together. What does it mean for you? How do we use this to make instruction as effective as possible? Let us summarize some points and add a few others.

The previous chapters have examined what goes on inside the trainee's head when skills are developed. This is mostly an automatic process, although most people also add to it a range of learning skills that can help. There is an important distinction to be made here and it is very relevant to instructors and the advice about instructing. Let us move back to the analogy of a tape recorder. Everyone knows that tape recorders do two things: they record sounds and they play them back. Both functions must work properly if the recorder is to be of any use at all. It is no good having recordings that you cannot play back and it is no use being able to play a blank tape on to which you cannot record anything. We use a learning machine to record our skills and, like the tape recorder, skill development has two aspects to it. We call the recording of skills learning and we call the playing back of the skill recording performance. In just the same way as with the tape recorder, we can only discover if skill recording has occurred by trying to play back the skill record; that is, we can only find out if learning has occurred by asking someone to perform. Unfortunately at this point we part company with the analogy of a tape recorder. In a tape recorder the record and play functions are very different. In people, however, learning occurs by performance – the two systems are mixed up and cannot be separated as cleanly as in a tape recorder. 'So what?', you might ask. Well, you, as instructor, can influence one part of the skill development process, but not the other – and that is one reason why much instructional advice in training is misleading.

Most, if not all, training books that discuss the theory of how people develop skill talk about learning theories – descriptions of how the skill recording process occurs. They then try to generate instructional advice around these theories. But that advice often does not work very well. The reason is that the learning process by which skills are recorded in the brain is an automatic, physiological process. It cannot be tinkered with directly (let's face it, it isn't even well understood by psychologists). What we can tinker with is the performance aspect of skill development. If you, as an instructor, can help the trainee to perform the skill at the right speed and in the right manner, then the automatic learning process will automatically record the skill for you. Instruction, therefore, is about helping trainees to perform properly (those of you who are academically inclined will find that theories of performance can be very helpful in generating useful instructional advice – see the bibliography given at the end of the chapter).

I started Chapter 5 by saying that we all have a powerful learning machine in our heads. Unfortunately the very power of the learning machine can cause problems. If the trainee performs the wrong actions then there is a real danger that those wrong actions will be learned. If the actions' speed is wrong then it may be that the actions will only ever be performed at the wrong speed. If we try to learn a skill at the top of the hierarchy of skills a lack of basic skill at the bottom may cause serious difficulty or failure. If we do not practise the skills in the proper way they will not develop. So, you must do things to help in all of these areas. But what you are really doing in instruction is smoothing the path for the learning machine to operate at its natural, rapid pace. When you make sure that the trainee only practises the right pattern of movements what is really happening is that the obstacles to learning those movements – all of the variations and wrong speeds – are being removed *before they arise*. Skill will then develop as rapidly as possible. When you think about the skill hierarchy and make sure that skills are learned in an appropriate sequence, the obstacles to rapid learning are being removed and the learning machine can record those skills without hindrance.

Correct performance of the skill is the gateway to learning. You can harness the power of the learning machine by removing the obstacles to correct performance. That is what effective instruction is all about. There is a range of instructional techniques that will help you to harness the learning machine's power and they are all techniques that work by making sure the trainee performs the skills properly right from the start of training (or as soon as possible). The following chapters describe those techniques.

Bibliography

Research focusing on instruction

Allison, M.G. and Ayllon, T. (1980), 'Behavioural coaching in the development of skills in football, gymnastics and tennis', *Journal of Applied Behaviour Analysis*, **13**, (2), 297–314.

Cox, J. (1933), 'Some Experiments on Formal Training in the Acquisition of Skill', *British Journal of Psychology*, **24**, 67–87.

Cratty, B.J. (1973), *Movement Behaviour and Motor Learning*, 3rd edn, Philadelphia: Lea and Febiger.

Crossman, E.R.F.W. (1959), 'A theory of the acquisition of speed skill', *Ergonomics*, **2**, 153–66.

Davies, D.R. (1945), 'The Effect of Tuition upon the Process of Learning a Complex Motor Skill', *Journal of Experimental Psychology*, **36**, 352–65.

Dusenberry, L. (1952), 'A Study of the Effects of Training in Ball Throwing by Children Aged Three to Seven', *Research Quarterly*, **23**, 9–14.

Flegg, D., Warren, A. and Law, C. (1982), *POISE: Project On Instructor Style and Effectiveness*, Cambridge: Industrial Training Research Unit Ltd.

Flegg, D. (1983), 'Developing Instructor Effectiveness – the P.O.I.S.E. approach', *Personnel Management*, May, 38–40.

Goodenough, F.L. and Brian, C.R. (1929), 'Certain Factors Underlying the Acquisition of Motor Skill by Pre-school Children', *Journal of Experimental Psychology*, **XII**, 127–55.

James, R. (1981), 'Learning and the instructor's role, Parts 1 and 2', *Journal of European Industrial Training*, **5**, (3), 23, (4), 17.

Martin, G. and Hrycaiko, D. (1983), 'Effective behavioural coaching: What's it all about?', *Journal of Sports Psychology*, **5**, (1), 8–20.

McGuinness, C. (1990), 'Talking About Thinking: The Role of Metacognition in Teaching Thinking', in Gilhooly, K.J., Keane, M.T.G., Logie, R.H. and Erdos, G. (eds), *Lines of Thinking*, Vol. 2, Chichester: John Wiley and Sons.

McGuinness, C. (1991), *Cognitive Apprenticeship: A Model of Instruction for Teaching Thinking*, paper to the British Psychological Society Annual Conference, Cognitive Section Symposium on Teaching Thinking, Bournemouth, April.

Newsham, D. and Fisher, J.M. (1972), 'What's in a style?', *Industrial and Commercial Training*, June, 291–5.

Newsham, D. (1976), *Choose an Effective Style*, research papers TR9 and TR11, Cambridge: Industrial Training Research Unit Ltd.

Patrick, J. (1992), *Training: Research and Practice*, London: Academic Press.

Pearcey, A.R.H. (1976), 'A Brief Description of Improved Machinist Training', *Bobbin*, September, 62 ff.

Pearcey, A.R.H. (1979), 'Developments in the Training of Sewing Machinists', *Training*, 9–15.

Rush, D.B. and Ayllon, T. (1984), 'Peer Behavioural Coaching: Soccer', *Journal of Sport Psychology*, **6**, 325–34.

Singer, R.N. (1977), 'To err or not to err: A question for the instruction of psychomotor skills', *Review of Educational Research*, **47**, (3), 479–98.

von Wright, J.M. (1957), 'A note on the role of "guidance" in learning', *Genetic Psychology*, **48**, (2), 133–7.

Wang, T.L. (1925), 'The Influence of Tuition in the Acquisition of Skill', *Psychological Monographs*, **34**, (1).

Whilden, P.P. (1956), 'Comparison of Two Methods of Teaching Beginning Basketball', *The Research Quarterly*, **27**, (2), 235–42.

Skills and skill development

Holding, D.H. (1965), *Principles of Training*, Oxford: Pergamon Press.

Holding, D.H. (ed.) (1989), *Human Skills*, 2nd edn, Chichester: John Wiley & Sons.

Robb, M.D. (1972), *The Dynamics of Motor-Skill Acquisition*, Englewood Cliffs, NJ: Prentice Hall.

The stages of skill acquisition

Anderson, J.R. (1982), 'Acquisition of Cognitive Skill', *Psychological Review*, **89**, (4), 369–406.

Anderson, J.R. (1987), 'Skill Acquisition: Compilation of Weak Method Problem Solving Solutions', *Psychological Review*, **94**, (2), 192–210.

Annett, J. (1991), 'Skill Acquisition', in Morrison, J.J. (ed.), *Training for Performance*, Chichester: John Wiley & Sons, 13–52.

Fitts, P.M. (1962), 'Factors in Complex Skill Training', in Glaser, R. (ed.), *Training Research and Education*, Chichester: John Wiley & Sons, 177–97.

Fitts, P.M. (1964), 'Perceptual motor-skill learning', in Melton, A.W. (ed.), *Categories of Human Learning*, New York: Academic Press.

The word brain and the body brain

Annett, J. (1991), 'Skill Acquisition', in Morrison, J.J. (ed.), *Training for Performance*, Chichester: John Wiley & Sons, 13–52.

Gallwey, W.T. (1974), *The Inner Game of Tennis*, London: Jonathan Cape.

Gallwey, W.T. (1979), *The Inner Game of Golf*, London: Jonathan Cape.

10

Designing skill practice conditions

Previous chapters have focused on the trainee's skill development and examined the implications of that for instruction. It is time to shift our focus on to the instructor, although we cannot ignore the trainee's internal process of skill development. We must always think about both together. This chapter explains how to design effective practice conditions in the light of skill development.

How you design the training process is central to the whole instructional task. The practice sequences are the context in which all the trainee's learning and skill development will occur as well as the context in which you will instruct. Do not forget that knowledge can be acquired by listening but doing can only ever be learned by doing. What the trainee does, how the trainee does it and how it all fits together must be designed before the training begins. If that design process goes wrong the skills will not develop easily, may take much longer to develop than is necessary and may not reach the necessary performance standards. It is possible to design exercises to:

- develop a trainee's physical resources (strength, stamina, flexibility, etc.);
- develop a trainee's mental resources (for example, memory, understanding and perceptual ability);
- develop knowledge which relates to a task;
- develop skill at a task.

In some cases a particular exercise may be developing several of those factors, in other cases an exercise may be focusing on just one of those factors. Getting the balance just right can be difficult, but why should this be? It comes back again to what the trainee's brain (and that means your brain as well) can do. We have seen in earlier chapters that the trainee has to work at holding the new skill or the new knowledge in his or her head. It has to be there for a while before the recording system can do its work and make the information a permanent part of the trainee's memory. We can understand this by thinking how hard it can be to remember a long shopping list. Our memory system can only hold so much at once. After that limit is reached, for every one new piece of new information that is added another one slips out – just like clothes from an overstuffed suitcase.

If the trainee is swamped in this way two things will happen. First, the memory contents will not transfer to permanent stores very well and, second, the trainee will not be able to control what is in the memory store at any one time and information will be lost at random. Hence the trainee's skill development will be erratic.

The trouble is, there are no simple rules for designing training practice. It is an art, and it is a difficult art for you to master. Each task and each training design must be taken on its own merits and the training practice conditions which you use to develop the trainee's skills must change and develop each time a trainee is trained. In this section we must think about two main areas: first, how to think through training practice and design your starting point and, second, how to develop that design over time and with experience. We will start with designing training practice and then think about developing and improving the design of the practice with experience.

Design of practice conditions flows from thinking about the task and what must be mastered to perform it properly. Many tasks are made up of a range of smaller tasks, some of which are more basic than the others. It makes sense to develop proficiency in the simpler and more basic tasks first. The problem is that it is not particularly easy to identify the different parts of the task jigsaw and then go on to put them into the best order for effective skill development. It can take many months of hard thought and less-than-perfect attempts before an effective training sequence is achieved. So, where do you start? Here is a rough map to help you navigate through the process.

Before you begin the process

Before you begin the long process of designing your own practice sequences, find out if anyone else has attempted to develop these particular skills before you. Many trainers borrow the ideas of other trainers and develop them. This has many advantages apart from being personally very convenient. Effective training is a living entity that many people must contribute to in various ways. If you can take someone else's foundation, identify weak areas and develop a better solution, in the long run everyone benefits – it will not be too long before someone else takes your approach and develops it further. If you find that there is little useful advice or examples from other sources, then you will have to make an attempt yourself to design the exercises and training sequence. Figure 10.1 summarizes a process which you can use. Let us look at that process in more detail.

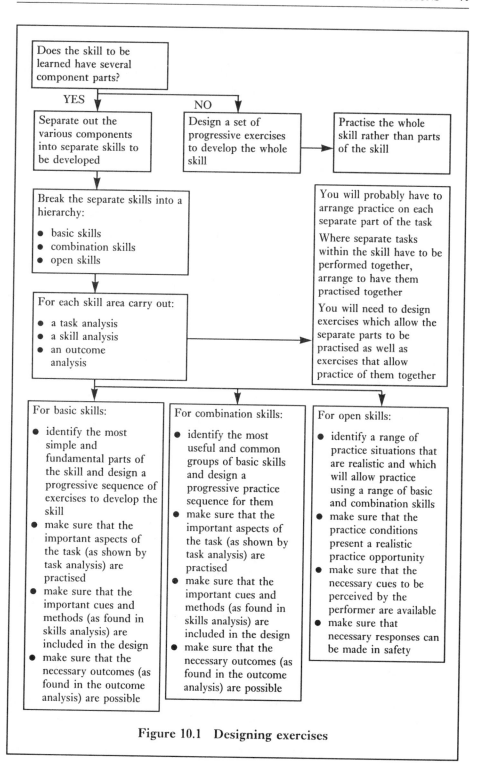

Figure 10.1   Designing exercises

Designing the practice sequence

The first stage of the design process is to ask if the skill has different component parts to it. If not, then the skill can be developed using a single sequence of progressive exercises specific to that one skill – a progressive sequence takes the most basic part of the skill as its start point and then, as the trainee gains mastery of that aspect, adds additional aspects of the task to the practice until they are all included. Deciding if the skill has several distinct parts to it can be a tricky decision to make as even a simple and seemingly cohesive skill can be broken into sub-sections if you try hard enough. If the task has several obvious and distinct parts it is best to design separate progressive exercise sequences for each part. Here is an example to illustrate the process of breaking a task down for training purposes. The example is drawn from industrial sewing.

Industrial sewing tasks are all very different. Take for example a sewing machinist whose job is to make a cocktail dress and compare her job with that of a sewing machinist whose job is to attach a collar on to a shirt. These tasks are very different even though both are sewing tasks. In the sewing world both are thought of as very difficult but for different reasons. Making a cocktail dress demands that the machinist can recognize the different pieces and sew them together in the right order so that they all fit together properly. Attaching a shirt collar is difficult because the neck of the shirt will vary in size and shape but must be fitted into the collar perfectly – the collar is a display area when the shirt is on sale and so it must look good. In addition, the machinist attaching the collar will have to complete the task in perhaps a minute and a half.

One of the sewing tasks is amenable to a single sequence of progressive exercises and one requires several sequences of progressive exercises to develop the different components of the whole task. Think about them both for a minute and then decide which task requires several exercise sequences and which requires one sequence of exercises.

Let us simplify things a lot in this example. Let us say that the shirt collar is attached to the shirt using one sewing seam about 20cm long. In contrast, the cocktail dress is put together using short seams (say, across the shoulders), medium-length seams (say, sewing darts in the waist area) and long seams (say, along the side of the dress from arm to hem). Now think about the two tasks and decide which one needs to have several exercise sequences to develop the skills.

The cocktail dress task would be more complex as different seam types and lengths would be used at different joins in the dress fabric. Each of the seam types would require a specific exercise sequence to develop the particular skills needed to construct that seam. Even sewing different-length seams requires different practice conditions because the fabric bulk for long seams needs to be controlled differently from the fabric in shorter seams. So the cocktail dress machinist would need to be trained to perform her task using several sequences of exercises to teach her to sew different seam types at differing lengths. Each exercise sequence would develop the skills needed to sew one seam type and one seam length. In contrast the collar machinist requires only one exercise sequence to develop the one-seam skill.

This example illustrates how a task can be broken down into component parts. There are several useful points which come out of it. First, not many people are familiar with sewing tasks (apart from amateur dressmakers, of course). That unfamiliarity is a drawback. Before you can begin to break a task down into component parts for training purposes you will need to understand the task fairly thoroughly. If you re-read the example you will see that it becomes easier to think about how to break the task down as you are given more information about it. That is another reason why it is very useful to perform task and skill analyses prior to training. Not only does that help you to describe the task to the trainee, it also helps you to prepare adequate training practice conditions.

The second point that can be made from the example is that thinking about a task for training purposes is not the same necessarily as thinking about it for production purposes. In the sewing industry it is common to try to teach sewing machinists using a view of the task that is more appropriate to describing the production process. For example, most people would describe the assembly of a cocktail dress in the following terms (or something like the following):

- Make the cuff.
- Attach the cuff to the sleeve.
- Join the shoulder seams.
- Attach the arms to the shoulders.
- Join the side seams starting at the cuff and continuing up the sleeve to the armpit and down the side of the garment.

And so on.

Now that is a good description of how to make a dress, but it is not a good description of the skills that are used to make the dress. The analysis is looking at the dress and not the sewing machinist. If we want to train someone to be able to do that task we must look at what the sewing machinist is doing when they make the dress. Here is the same task from an instructing point of view:

- Make the cuff – sew a short flat (two pieces of fabric joined with no folds) seam with two tight curves, within 4 mm of the edge of the fabric.
- Attach the cuff to the sleeve – sew a short flat seam within 4 mm of the edge of the fabric, joining three pieces of fabric.
- Attach the front and back at the shoulder – sew two short flat seams within 4 mm of the edge of the fabric to join two pieces of fabric.
- Attach the sleeve to the shoulder – sew a long (30 cm) seam joining two curved pieces of fabric where the curves run in opposite directions, within 4 mm of the edge of the fabric.

- Close the side seams, from the cuff to the armpit and down the side of the dress – sew a very long seam (90 cm) to join two pieces of fabric within 4 mm of the edge of the fabric.

And so on

That is a better description of the skills used to perform the task, and using this method it becomes much easier to break the practice down into separate sequences. In this case there is a lot of overlap of skill across the different tasks but it seems likely that several exercise sequences will be necessary to develop the complete range of skills. Sewing a short seam with tight curves (making the cuff) is not very like sewing a long seam along the side of the dress, so the two tasks may need separate practice conditions and exercise sequences. What other, if any, exercise sequences would you like to include?

The third point that comes from this example is that, as the different exercise sequences are used to develop the range of skills needed, there will be a carry-over from one to the next. Thus, as the new trainee develops skill at sewing a long seam we can expect some carry-over to the sewing of a short seam. We could expect therefore that fewer exercises would be needed to develop the second skill and that performance would grow more quickly than had the trainee started from a position of no skill at all.

After you have designed your various progressive exercise sequences for the individual skills it is worth standing back to consider if some of the skills cluster together in such a way that it would be useful to practise them all together. If possible, try to capitalize on the skills the trainee has already developed and use them if you can to help the trainee develop any additional skills more quickly.

The skills hierarchy and the design of practice conditions

In Chapter 7 we pointed out that complex tasks are made up of a skill hierarchy, where simple or basic skills are combined into groups and the groups are applied to the changing environment. Because each of these levels was a skill of a different nature from the other levels, the skills at each level of the hierarchy required slightly different approaches for their effective development. In the example above we have chosen a task that can be performed in a very closed fashion. Unlike an ice-hockey player, the sewing machinist seldom has to fend off the attacks of competing sewing machinists as she sews, and the sewing machine seldom moves about in an unpredictable way as she sews. So her environment is stable and she does not have to modify what she does to take account of an unpredictable workplace. Many skills are not like that. Instead of being closed they are open skills – driving a car is a good example. We drive through changing conditions, subject to the seemingly random actions of hormone-crazed adolescent drivers, lemming-like pedestrians and other dangerous denizens of the road.

If we are to develop effective practice conditions for our trainees we must take the skills hierarchy into account. For many (but not all) sewing machinists we can note the skills hierarchy and promptly forget it. For other tasks we must use the ideas underlying the skills hierarchy to identify how to order our training practice. It makes little sense to teach high-level skills (perceiving and reacting to the environment) if the trainee lacks the basic skilled responses. Imagine trying to teach a learner driver to navigate through a rush hour on their first lesson! It makes more sense to allow them to practise stopping and starting, turning left and right, going faster and slower, and so on before allowing them to face the lunatics they will be sharing the road system with.

If the task you are to teach must be broken down into a range of component skills, you must think about the various skills that it breaks down into – we have illustrated that process above. As you do that, make sure that you think about which of those skills are basic skills that can be or should be practised first and possibly practised separately from the others. Think about which, if any, of those skills need to be grouped together and need to be practised as groups. If there are some, think which groups are more basic and consider teaching those first. Finally, you will have to think about providing some real-life practice that will allow the trainee to perceive and react to the changing world and to apply the basic and combination skills which they have developed with your help. That real-life practice is a skill development exercise in its own right and will need to be treated as one.

Fitting the practice exercises together

The final point to make about designing a sequence of practice exercises and conditions is concerned with fitting the different skills together. There has been a debate within academic circles for many years about the relative value of part training and whole training. The debate concerns whether it is better to practise the whole task or to practise parts of the task separately and then practise with the parts put together. As you might expect, the answer is that both are useful according to the circumstances. For example, where a task is made up of a skill that is coherent and difficult to separate into smaller tasks it makes sense to try to teach it as one coherent whole. There is a problem with this, however. Even a simple skill may need to be simplified further so that a totally unskilled trainee can practise key elements of the task and then move on to a slightly more complex version of the task, before attempting the whole task. That is the progressive exercise sequence and it works very well in the appropriate circumstances. But what if the skill is coherent and difficult to separate, and is very complex? Will the trainee be able to practise the task as a whole? Probably not, and under those circumstances it may be useful to try emphasizing some of the more simple aspects of the task in the early stages of training before moving on to less simple aspects as the trainee masters the early practice tasks. An example of this is driving.

All the different tasks that make up driving are usually performed in a very integrated way by skilled drivers. It therefore makes very good sense to try to practise the skills in that same, integrated fashion. But, in driving, some tasks are more difficult than others, so it is better for a learner to practise the simple tasks first, in a safe and undemanding environment (for example, stopping, starting, and simple manoeuvres on a test track). As they master those simple tasks they can move on to practise in undemanding traffic conditions (the typical Sunday morning learner driver). As their skill develops new and more difficult tasks (reversing) can be introduced as they drive around. As they master those tasks, they can begin to face progressively more demanding traffic conditions. Thus the driving task is being practised in a progressive fashion but also in the same integrated fashion during training as it must be performed when training is finished.

At no point in a well-designed progressive sequence will the trainee be overwhelmed and unable to develop skill as a result. And, in a well-designed exercise sequence, you will be able to guide and instruct so as to help the trainee avoid error and to practise only the correct methods and procedures.

Some tasks are not amenable to the progressive-but-integrated approach to developing skill. The nature of the task or the nature of the materials or resources may mean that parts of the task must be practised separately before they can be practised together. In itself that is not a problem. Difficulties sometimes arise when the instructor forgets to allow the trainee to practise the various parts in combination. By all means arrange for the separate parts of the task to be practised separately until a degree of skill is attained, but then arrange to have the different parts practised together. Let us go back to the example we used earlier – making a dress – to illustrate this.

Making a dress often requires the machinist to be able to sew many different seam types on a range of fabrics that curve and stretch in different ways. In real life it is not practical to have the trainee practise on dresses that are intended for sale. It is too expensive and they will be overwhelmed by the difficulty and complexity of the task. It makes sense to have the trainee learn to sew different seams on practice exercises – pieces of fabric that can be discarded when they have been used. These skills will be practised separately. But at some point the trainee will have to move on to more complex combinations of the seam types, combinations that are very similar to the real task. These combinations have to be treated as practice sessions in just the same way as did the individual seams. The combination practice acts as a transition between basic skills on disposable fabric and doing the job for real. Without practice at putting the various seams together on practice materials the leap between basic sewing and production-line sewing will be too great and the trainee will often fail to bridge the gap.

Practice design: summary

Let us summarize what you have to do when designing practice conditions for the first time. First you will have to understand the task from a skills point of view, that is, what the performer does at different stages of the task. You will then have to ask yourself if the task has separate component parts that are sufficiently different to be practised separately before being practised in combination. If the task is a closely integrated and cohesive task which cannot be broken into component parts, arrange for the trainee to practise it as an integrated whole – although you may have to think about ways of designing a simplified version of the task with progressively more aspects of the task being built into a progressive practice sequence.

For tasks that can be separated into component parts, ask yourself if some parts of the task are more basic than others and arrange to have those practised first. If some basic elements are performed in combination, ask yourself which combinations are most common and arrange practice of those combinations first.

When the task to be learned has an open element, arrange for practice in changing conditions so that the trainee has a chance to practise reacting to the changing environment, but try to make sure that the trainee is not overwhelmed with too much change too soon. You may have to arrange for a series of controlled practice sessions which limit the amount of change to which the trainee has to react so that the trainee has the opportunity to practise usefully rather than freeze in dismay.

Developing the training conditions with experience

The practice conditions you design will not be perfect on the first attempt. They will have to be redesigned and modified with successive trainees until you have achieved a training design that works very well most times. It may seem to be a rather obvious point to make, but many trainers and instructors design a series of practice conditions and then fail to consider that they could be improved. It is also sadly true that the practice conditions are not always well designed in the first place, for a range of reasons. While it may be understandable that time pressure or resource limitations can result in a set of practice exercises that are less than ideal, there is not much excuse for failing to think of ways to improve them over time. Perhaps it is just that most instructors do not know where to start changing them and how.

Unfortunately there are no simple rules for developing better exercise sequences. The only realistic approach is to evaluate the results you achieve from the current practice conditions and compare those results with the occasional redesign. Do not try to change everything completely. Instead, change one or two aspects of the practice you currently use and see what improvement it makes. If the practice conditions you use now are fairly useful, try to build on what you have rather than change it completely. Then measure the results you achieve from the new design to see if it is an improvement on how you did it before – you will need to know a little about evaluating training to do that. Here is an example of how an exercise sequence can be developed for the better, continuing with the theme of sewing.

Some years ago the UK sewing industry was served by a national training body, the Clothing and Allied Products Industry Training Board (C&APITB). This body trained many instructors within the industry and as a part of that training helped instructors to devise exercises and practice sequences for the trainee sewing machinists. Instructors who attended the C&APITB instructor training finished the programme able to design exercises that started with a new trainee and finished with a skilled sewing machinist. Over the years that the instructor training was carried out, C&APITB was able to show that training times in many factories within the industry had been cut from months to weeks. The training exercises that the instructors developed obviously worked very well, but that did not mean that development was not possible. Before we can describe what that development was, we will have to describe briefly what the instructors did when they developed training exercises.

On the C&APITB instructor programme instructors were trained to break down a sewing job into its component parts and decide which of those component parts were simple and basic, which less simple, and so on. At the end of this process there would be a progressive sequence of exercises which the sewing trainee could use to develop skill in that particular sewing job. The first exercise in the sequence was very often to pick up, position and sew two pieces of fabric and then lay the joined pieces aside. That sounds easy enough, but the trainee had to perform this task at speed, and an industrial sewing machine sews very much faster than a domestic machine. The new trainee was often frightened by the machine and lacked control skills. That had an adverse effect on the sewing that they did. So, although the first exercise in the training sequence was nearly always intended to develop a simple fabric-handling skill (pick up, position, sew, lay aside), in reality it was also developing machine control and confidence as well as sewing skills. The lack of confidence and lack of machine control skills interfered with the fabric-handling practice. What would you do in these circumstances? What do you think is needed?

If you think about it, being able to control the sewing machine safely and confidently is a more basic skill than is the fabric handling involved in sewing. Without the one you cannot do the other, so it made sense to devise some practice exercises which would develop machine control skills that could be used by any sewing trainee. Let us see what was developed.

A sewing machine is fairly straightforward to control. It stops and it starts, maybe sometimes it needs to sew slowly, but more often (because of production requirements) it must be used at full speed. Indeed, the quality of the sewn seams is often better if they are sewn at full speed because the speed constrains the possible fabric-handling variations. The following series of machine control exercises were therefore designed:

1. A length of fabric was looped so that it could be run through an un-threaded sewing machine operating at full speed. The trainee's task was to control the fabric so that it ran under the needle all the time. This exercise developed familiarity with the machine running at full speed as well as introducing the basics of fabric guiding during full-speed sewing.
2. A similar loop of fabric was used but lines were drawn across the fabric at regular intervals reflecting the sewing lengths that the trainee would be sewing on the production task. The trainee's task with this loop was to sew at full speed, guide the fabric under the needle (continuing practice from the first exercise) but also to stop the machine (using the machine's brake) on the lines. This exercise developed stopping and starting skills.
3. The trainee's task was to join together at one edge two long, narrow pieces of fabric and sew along the edge using the machine at full speed in one burst of sewing.

The effect of these exercises was very dramatic. Nervous trainees who had never before used an industrial sewing machine became very expert at using one at full speed within half an hour. Often, as a result of their focused practice, their sewing speed was faster than that of experienced machinists. Whereas the experienced machinists had learned to sew slowly and then speed up, the trainees who had practised machine control at full speed were slowing down to the desired speeds when they came to practise the task exercises – a very useful result.

These exercises became standard throughout the industry and, in use, always preceded the sewing exercises, designed by the instructor, that were job-specific. The outcome of using the machine control exercises was that the trainees began their task training with complete control of the sewing machine, able to operate it with confidence at full speed. As a result the task-specific skills were usually developed very quickly and easily. The early machine control exercises had removed the element of machine control from every sub-sequent sewing task exercise that the instructors designed, which meant that instead of learning both task skills and machine control skills on each practice exercise the trainees were learning just the sewing skills of fabric handling – machine control was already present.

This example illustrates how improvements to exercise and practice designs can be made. Before development and improvement can take place, however, you must be willing to think about what you are doing and ask if it can be improved. If that willingness is absent, development will not occur. Let us sum-marize the main points about developing and improving practice sequences:

• Be willing to consider how your exercise sequences and practice conditions can be improved.
• Do not try to change everything at once. Try to identify key points and change those first.
• Measure how effective your training is before you change anything. If you do not measure what you do you have no control over what is happening.

11

Preparing for instruction

As we have said before, instruction does not just happen. Effective instruction is a carefully planned process, and the plan that you use has to be carefully controlled at every point along the trainee's route from raw novice to fully skilled performer. In this chapter we outline the preparation and planning that has to be undertaken before instruction can occur.

In many ways instruction concerns putting training plans into action – if there is no plan, there will not be much useful action. As an effective instructor you will be preparing for most of the following points, maybe even a few more than are listed here. Use these lists as a basis from which to develop your own pre-instruction checklists. When you prepare to instruct you will have to make some arrangements or carry out work in most of the following areas:

- You must understand the task you are to instruct.
- You must plan the structure of the practice sessions: knowledge and practice exercises.
- You must select the right trainee.
- You must prepare the trainee for the training.
- You must prepare the organization to receive trainees.
- You must prepare the equipment and raw materials.
- You must prepare the instruction methods.

In many instructing situations you will be carrying out the same form of instruction over and over again – in a training school, perhaps, where the training cycle is repeated every few weeks or months. In that case, much of this pre-instruction preparation will be carried out once only at the start of the whole process. After that initial flurry of activity the pre-instruction tasks are largely routine and low key. Other instructors or coaches may base their instruction on plans provided in books or on coaching training courses. They will not do much preparation themselves – someone else will have done it for them. As a result, they will not have the opportunity to become skilled at these preparation activities. They may underrate both the importance and the usefulness of pre-instruction preparation. More importantly, perhaps, these instructors may never question whether the preprepared instructional practices they do use are the best at the time they are using them. One example of this is the mythology about effective selling techniques that were used to train many thousands of salespeople around the world for many years – as we described in the Preface, the traditional sales techniques were ineffective!

What this means for you is that you should become familiar with these pre-instruction planning points. Take some time to think through what they mean in your particular context and ask if your instructing situation is well planned and prepared. Let us take each of the points in turn and briefly draw out some of the main items that you must consider.

You must understand the task you are to instruct

Being able to understand the task is not the same as being able to do the task, but it is the same as being able to describe it in detail. Many instructors in industry are made into instructors because they are very good operators. The logic behind this is that if you are a good performer on the job you must also be the best person to teach others to do that job. But that is not necessarily true. A good instructor will have mastered the training techniques that help him or her to understand what aspects of the job are important and to understand what the job consists of *from a training point of view*. Ideally, if you are able to investigate and analyse a task so as to be able to teach it, you will be able to apply those pre-instructional analysis skills to any task and will therefore be able to understand that task from an instructing point of view. But knowing what are the key points of the task, what cues to watch for, how to react in certain situations, what movements to make and how to make them – all aspects of knowing the job – does not mean you will be able to do the task. Understanding the task will help you to:

- describe the task to the trainee;
- identify what actions (mental or physical) you must help the trainee to perform;
- identify the knowledge that is necessary for correct performance of the task;
- pinpoint when specific actions (mental or physical) must occur if the task is to proceed properly;
- specify what counts as adequate performance in terms of speed and accuracy, both as the task is performed and when the task is finished.

Let us expand this basic list to show you in more detail what you must know (and preferably have recorded in writing) before you can begin to teach the task. To understand a task fully you will probably need to be able to describe to the trainee most of the following task details:

- the sequence of operations or actions that are a part of the task;
- the key points that must be performed in a specific way;
- any tricks of the trade for each aspect of the task;
- how to lay out work pieces ready for efficient working – that is, use the most efficient movement patterns;
- how to prepare for performing the task;
- how to maintain or look after the equipment that is used;
- how to perform the task with due regard for safety;
- the cues that must be attended to or watched for by the trainee: how to recognize them when they occur;
- how to react if and when certain events happen;
- what not to do if certain events happen;
- the precise methods (procedures or operations for mental or decision tasks, movements and handling methods for movement tasks) that must be used and the points in the task sequence at which they must be used;
- the expected outcomes of the task at key points within the task and at the end of the task;
- the speed at which the task must be performed overall;
- the quality standards that will be used and that must be adhered to;
- how to tell if things are going wrong and what to do or how to recover if things go wrong.

The list is not exhaustive and it cannot be comprehensively applied to every task. Some tasks will demand some points are covered, other tasks will demand different points are covered. You will have to use the list as a basis for devising your own checklists. You will be surprised at just how much information you have to give to the trainee in the course of developing even a simple skill. Obtaining this information is called task analysis.

Task analysis is the range of techniques that you use to help you understand the task that you have to help the trainee perform. Some tasks are mostly mental in nature (for example, the tasks of a counter clerk in a bank), other tasks are more movement-oriented (for example, sewing or swimming). Some tasks are a mixture of mental and physical. Whatever the components you must determine exactly what elements go to make up the complete task and you must do that before you begin to plan your instruction. It is only when you know what the task involves that you can begin to plan the necessary demonstrations, explanations and practice sessions. There are many excellent books which give you very detailed explanations of how to go about task analysis for a wide range of differing tasks – thinking tasks, doing tasks and all combinations of the two.

You must select the right trainee

There are a number of occasions in training when it is necessary to select the trainee very carefully. For example, it isn't just anyone who gets to fly a fighter aircraft. Trainees are selected on a wide range of physical characteristics that predict who is most likely to be able to complete the training and finish with the aircraft intact. In industry, applicants for training may have to have certain academic achievements to show they can cope with the intellectual rigours of the training or the job, or they may be required to take part in a trainability test to show they can learn easily. In amateur sport it is not unusual for a coach to be faced with trainees with a wide range of abilities and aptitudes who all want to play in the game on Saturday. It would not be wise (or fair) to be too selective because there is always a danger that there will not be a team to play if only the very best are selected. But if the training sessions are particularly intense a form of self-selection may operate where aspiring team members who find it too demanding may stop coming to the training sessions.

Selection itself is a very large topic that could fill and indeed has filled many books and formed the basis of many training courses. This book is not concerned with the detail of the selection procedures as such. Instead, the aim of this section is to alert you to the fact that it is possible, often desirable, to select your trainees carefully. There are many advantages to selecting your trainees and there are many ways of selecting for training. But why should you wish to select trainees in the first place? The most common answers are:

- For safety reasons: for example, drivers may have to demonstrate that they have adequate eyesight.
- For cost reasons: for example, trainees within industry whose trainability test suggests they may require additional instructional effort to achieve performance will tie up expensive instructor resource. If their training period is longer than average it will cost their employer more to train them. Trainees who start a period of training but who are unable successfully to complete the training will be a very costly drain on the company's training and recruitment resources. Fighter pilots must be very carefully selected because a failure during training will cost lives as well as an expensive aircraft.
- To avoid personality clashes: for example, élite athletes rely on their coaches to help them prepare for competition and hone their skills. At this level of training it is important that both trust each other completely. The athlete needs to feel that the coach is able to help and is working for his or her best interests. The coach needs to feel that he or she has the complete trust of the athlete. From time to time the sports press will report a split between a top athlete and his or her coach. Often one underlying reason is that the element of trust between them has gone.

Trainees can be selected for a range of factors that impinge on their ability to achieve performance during training. This list is not exhaustive, it merely illustrates some of the factors that can be important pre-requirements for some training schemes:

- physical strength and stamina, as well as physical abilities (running, throwing, etc.);

- good health;
- adequate sensory abilities;
- academic ability;
- ability to retain instructions and apply them;
- ability to work in a team;
- ability to operate under pressure or stress;
- willingness to stay the distance during training;
- compatibility with the coach/instructor.

There are two main points to bear in mind when selecting trainees for training that relate to the use of selection procedures:

- Make sure that you do not discriminate unfairly when you select: the aim of selection is to help discriminate between several individuals. You will want to be able to differentiate between them and choose those that are best suited to your purposes. However, it is important to avoid unfair discrimination on the grounds of factors that have no relationship between their performance in training and on the job.
- Make sure that the selection procedures you use are valid and reliable measures wherever possible. A valid measure is one that really does measure what it purports to, a reliable measure will produce a similar result on several re-measures. Most respectable and useful assessment and selection procedures have been carefully designed and researched to make sure they are both valid and reliable indicators. In contrast, rule-of-thumb measures that an individual thinks up and uses may be very misleading and unfair. At best such measures will deny training to the prospective trainee, at worst they may deny that person employment.

If you want to select trainees to make sure that they can be trained cost-effectively you will have to research to find out if there is a selection procedure suitable for that skill. There are many professionals who will be able to give you advice on which test to use. It may be that there isn't a selection procedure in existence for you to use, in which case you may have to think about designing one yourself. There are five basic steps to this:

1. *Identify what counts as success in the particular task to be trained.* You will need to be able to identify successful performance on the task. Training success may be based on cost factors, safety and ease of training as well as whether trainees manage to achieve the task's performance criteria. Success is a balance between achieving the task's performance criteria and the effort and expense it took to get the trainee to do that. When you can describe successful performance you can begin to identify what factors make up the task skill, and those are factors that you will need to measure in your prospective trainees.

2. *Identify what qualities and abilities of the trainee are necessary if they are to achieve training success in the shortest possible time and with (relatively) the*

least training effort. This is almost impossible to do in advance – in the absence of detailed training and personal information about the trainees it becomes little more than guesswork. How can that problem be overcome? In many cases selection can be based on simple characteristics such as ability to read and write. Sometimes it is enough to know something about the applicant's background – perhaps the applicant has relatives and family members who have performed the same job. For many sporting tasks it is enough that the trainee expresses an interest – not everyone wants to be an Olympic-class athlete and for those who do the years of practice and competition act as their own selection process. For many other industrial and commercial tasks dedication and willingness are not always enough. There remains a requirement to identify who will become proficient most easily, quickly and cheaply. For these tasks there is a continuing need for selection procedures. So how do you go about finding out the characteristics that can be used to predict training success? In practice the simplest way is to keep records of all trainees who have ever been trained on the task and look to see who was trained most quickly to performance criteria. If you also have information about their individual characteristics, for example physical abilities, academic achievements, personality types, interests and hobbies, and so on, you may be able to tease out factors that are useful indicators of training success. However, this is complicated by changes in training methods. Suppose training methods have changed, the people who were most successful before the changes may be very different from those who were successful following the changes. Further change may have a similar effect. Sophistication in selection is most likely to be successful and useful where the task has very clear underlying requirements that are independent of variation in the task or in the training methods used (for example, flying fighter aircraft or running a marathon – both tasks make particular physical and mental demands on the individuals performing them and it is these physical and mental characteristics that become important in selection). It is almost certain that sophisticated selection will be based on many years of research and development. Development of even a simple scheme in industry may need to be based on very careful research over a period of time, and so it represents a considerable investment. For example, in the UK clothing industry research carried out by the Industrial Training Research Unit found that most traditional trainee selection methods in use at the time were completely useless at predicting who would do well in training and who would not. They found that the best predictor was the trainee's ability to learn, and tests (trainability tests) were developed that allowed companies to select those trainees most likely to learn to do their tasks in the shortest time and to the highest standards. However, even this test had limitations – it required a good training system to support the characteristics that it used as the basis of selection.

3. *Produce some form of assessment that will accurately and fairly test the training candidates on the qualities and abilities that are deemed to be useful indicators*

of training success. Once you have an idea of what factors lead to success in training you will need to develop a procedure for assessing those factors in potential trainees. Developing assessment procedures can be as difficult as identifying on what characteristics to base your selection. In many cases, though, a carefully structured interview will be perfectly adequate. More formal and objective tests can be, and are, used for selecting trainees. For example, trainability tests can be designed for a range of tasks and there are many other forms of attainment tests, ability and aptitude tests available commercially. However, it is worth pointing out that some psychologists have been worried that many of these tests are being used to make profit for the test producer rather than because they are really useful as selection devices. There are many other psychologists who defend the use of such tests for selection purposes. In addition, there is an issue about how well such tests and assessments are applied by the test user. The British Psychological Society has recently produced a qualification for test users in industry and commerce which it is hoped will reduce the incidence of poor practice and the use of inappropriate tests for selection.

4. *Keep full training records to help you to review the relationship between trainees' training progress and the characteristics you have identified as being important success indicators.* Should you have decided to implement some form of selection process and gone through the process of identifying the success criteria, identifying the characteristics that predict success in training and obtaining assessment procedures, you will want to try it out. It is tempting to think that after all of that effort it will be enough to simply apply it and use it. Not so. Even after all that effort it may not work as well as you hoped it would. You will have to try it out in a carefully designed implementation trial. How does that operate? First of all you will need to have your new selection system designed and ready. You will then apply both your old selection system and the new selection system to trainees as they apply for training. You will need to have two groups of at least 40 trainees for at least two training programmes. That number of trainees and two programmes helps to correct for random variations in trainees and training that may lead to a biased outcome. You will need to keep adequate training records for each trainee. At the end of training you will compare the predictions of the old selection system with the new selection system to see how well each procedure predicts training success. Hopefully the new system will be better than the old. If so, you can proceed with the final step – step 5.

5. *Implement the new system.* If you are sure that the new selection system is giving you good predictions about who will benefit most from training and who will be trained most quickly and easily, then it is time for a full implementation of the system. However, just because a system is now in everyday use, that does not mean that you should not monitor its effectiveness on a regular basis. As we noted above, changes in training methods, changes in the task being taught and changes in the nature of the candidates applying for training may mean that the selection system slowly

drifts away from effectiveness. You will need to monitor the results and, if necessary, redesign the selection process.

You must prepare the trainee for the training

In addition to the task-related skills and knowledge, the trainee also needs a clear understanding of the task as it fits into the context in which they will be working. As well as the task knowledge the trainee also needs information on the associated role and responsibilities that go with the task, the chains of command and who can give orders and who cannot, other people's roles and responsibilities in relation to the trainee's, the organization's procedures and processes, the expected outcomes from the trainee's performance and how that influences other workmates doing their job, and so on.

This sort of information is an extension of any induction programme (an induction programme is an introduction to the organization and related information about the job, hours of work, wage payment arrangements, fire drills, toilets, etc.). It is directly relevant to the way in which the trainee will perform the job and may help or hinder performance on the job. It makes sense to prepare this information in advance.

When is the best time to tell the trainee about all this? Almost inevitably there will be times in training when the trainee is tired and needs a rest. It is bad practice to insist on a tired trainee continuing to work – all that will happen is that they will learn to perform the task in a tired fashion. So, fill the practice rest breaks with useful information.

Preparing the trainee for training

You will want the trainee to work with you as you instruct. One way of encouraging an alert and positive attitude on the part of the trainee is to prepare them for what is to come:

- Introduce yourself.
- Explain how you will be working with the trainee and what your role is.
- Explain to the trainee what their role in training is to be, what you expect from them and what they can expect from you.
- Explain the training process that is about to occur.
- Ask if they have any questions at this point.

Some of this material will have to be prepared in advance, especially if you have not trained anyone in this task before. It can be useful to have a checklist available to use as a prompt so that you do not forget anything. Do not forget the trainee will be anxious and probably will not take in much information as a result. Keep what you say simple and be prepared to answer questions and to explain the training process again.

You must prepare the organization to receive trainees

The transfer from training to the workplace can be difficult for the trainee. Trainees in industry are not only learning a new task but also have to cope with new workmates, new rules and a new organization. In some sports a new team member may need to be trained, but then he or she has to join the team. It makes sense to think through how to integrate the new person with the organization or team they are about to join. In part that can be done prior to training by the preparation you build into the training programme, and in part it can be helped by you following up the trainee after they have left training for the workplace.

What sort of points should you be looking for when you examine the workplace to see if it is ready to accept the trainee? Let us look at it from the trainee's point of view:

- *The right skills to do the job.* For many industrial and commercial tasks there are specific task skills that allow the trainee to do the immediate job. But there are often other skills which are equally important that help the trainee to do the job well. For example, a building society employee or a bank employee may have been trained to deal with the technical side of their job but they also talk to customers face to face and on the telephone. There may be a need for effective telephone technique, customer contact skills, communication skills, and so on. These, more peripheral, skills are as important to performing the task well as the more central skills of being able to identify the most appropriate mortgage or insurance arrangements for the client. The main point here is that the skills needed to do the job are all the things that the person must be able to do effectively, not just the technical skills. You will have to prepare the full training package in advance. Sometimes the workplace functions in a way that is different from how the trainee is being taught to work – training is out of step with the organization. Sometimes the organization's culture is out of step with the correct procedures: 'That's all very well, son. They may tell you to do it like that in the training school, but we do it this way down here!' You will need to investigate if this happens and try to correct it, either in the training programme or by management action in the workplace.
- *The right information to do the job in a form that is accessible and easily understood.* It is not enough to just give complex technical information to the trainees and staff and leave it up to them to sort it all out – although, unfortunately, that often happens. The information should be presented in a way that helps trainees to understand what it is about and helps trainees to use it easily on the job as well as helping trainees to remember it all. However, the information requirements of most jobs go beyond the obvious technical information. Trainees will often need to know a wide range of other information if they are to perform their job effectively. For example, who is the appropriate person to deal with particular queries, who or where

to access particular sources of help, what to do in specific situations, how to solve common customer difficulties, how to proceed when a customer has an uncommon difficulty, and so on.

- *The equipment to do the job, ready to be used.* If a trainee is to perform effectively on the job the equipment has to be ready to be used. This applies to training equipment as well as job equipment. Equipment is a broad term that includes soft equipment (forms, technical manuals, and so on) as well as mechanical equipment. Mechanical equipment should be properly set up, fully functional and ready to use. Soft equipment, such as paper-based or information technology (IT) equipment and software should be functional (that is, it should do the job it was designed to do) and it should also be usable – if the forms, IT systems, and so on are not user-friendly the staff will have difficulty using them properly. Not only will the function be impaired, so will staff effectiveness and learning to do the job will be more difficult than it needs to be.

- *The time to do the job properly.* A trainee's effectiveness may be impaired if they have too many tasks to do at differing levels of responsibility. It may make sense to limit what they have to do at first, to give them time to master part of the task before they are introduced to other parts of the job. You will have to plan this process of introduction before the trainee begins to train.

Clearly some of the items in this list are personal to the individual job and trainee – for example, the task-related skills and knowledge. Some of the items are more organizational in nature. An individual's skills and knowledge or willingness to do the task are either present or not present. When they are present the task can be performed.

Organizational issues, in contrast, are always present and can either work to help the individual perform the task or work to hinder the task's performance. Organizational issues are more difficult to change than are individual issues that reduce performance on the task. Trainees often fail to perform well following transfer to the workplace because organizational problems hinder their job performance. If this happens it is important to be able to identify that it is the organization that is at fault and not the trainee or their skills. Use the trouble-shooting chart (Figure 11.1) to help you decide what the problem is and what to do about it.

It is particularly important that the trainee has supportive colleagues and that the system they work within helps them to apply the skills they need to have. You should consider arranging follow-up for trainees after they have left the training area. This helps them by offering a friendly and well-known face for them to tell their problems to. It offers you the chance to find out what is really going on at the place of work – you may need to change your training or to try to change the work practices so that the trainee can apply their skills effectively. You will need to plan, or at least think about, your follow-up procedures before training begins.

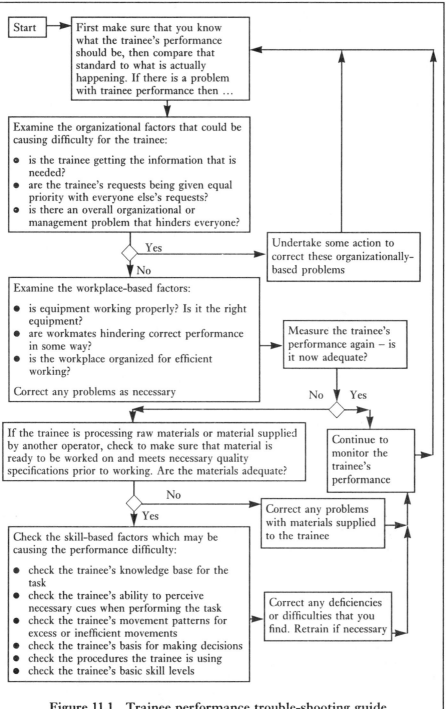

Figure 11.1   Trainee performance trouble-shooting guide

You must prepare the equipment and raw materials needed for training

You will have to prepare the equipment that the trainee needs to be able to use. Ideally, the equipment (either soft equipment or mechanical) that is used in training will be identical to that used in the workplace. Any differences in the equipment will cause the trainee unnecessary difficulty as they learn to use new equipment on the job. Any equipment that the trainee uses should be set up to be safe and it is essential that full safety instruction is given. The equipment will also need to be in full working order, properly set up to do the job and ready to use. Regular maintenance, preferably preventive maintenance that keeps the machine in full working order rather than breakdown maintenance, is needed. Faulty equipment means the trainee cannot practise properly!

You will need to prepare training for the trainee that tells them how to use the equipment safely and effectively. Typical areas to be prepared are:

- how to operate the equipment or how to make use of it;
- how to start up and shut down;
- how to clean and care for the equipment;
- basic trouble-shooting and problem identification;
- if possible and necessary, basic maintenance of simple problems or appropriate procedures in the event of a breakdown; for example, what to do when a problem is detected, who to tell and what to do until help arrives.

You must prepare the instruction methods

So far we have described briefly some of the more important areas of pre-instruction preparation that you will need to carry out, but these have been *what* to include in your training, or *what* training practice to arrange. We have yet to cover *how* you are going to instruct, and one of the most important areas of preparation for you is your instruction methods. You will need to think through how to convey the knowledge needed by the trainee and how to arrange and conduct the action-based instruction.

There are various methods of passing on knowledge to trainees, for example lectures, demonstrations, hand-outs and manuals, role-play sessions, conferences, self-instruction manuals, audio tapes, film and video tapes, and so on. They all have their good points and bad points for both the instructor and the trainee. There are many books and articles available to explain about passing on knowledge effectively – we have listed some at the end of this chapter which will help you to explore the various methods in more detail. In this book we are more concerned with how to develop skilled actions.

Preparing instruction to develop skilled actions is less easy than preparing to give knowledge to trainees. Perhaps that is why it is seldom mentioned in training books. Why is it so difficult to prepare? For one reason, it is not a good idea to produce a script for helping trainees to do things. Recent research has found that effective instructors do not script what they say to trainees during skill practice. Instead, effective instructors vary what they say to trainees as the situation demands; they are flexible. Ineffective instructors, on the other hand, do script out their instruction to trainees. Not only that, ineffective instructors do not vary what they say, or how much they say as their trainees gain skill. Effective instructors, on the other hand, vary not only the content of what they say but also their style of talking and the amount of talking as the trainee's skills develop. There is a more detailed outline of this in the next chapter. For now, these findings suggest that it is not a good idea to prepare a script for your activity instruction. That does not mean there is no preparation you can do for helping your trainees develop their skill. As we have mentioned above, you can prepare the following:

- a detailed knowledge of what you want your trainees to do and how they should do it;
- a clear idea of what your trainees will need to know to be effective;
- a planned sequence of skill practice;

and, most importantly, you can make sure that you have an adequate amount of time to carry out the instruction. Plan to spend most of your time with the trainee, especially in the early stages of skill development. The reasons for this are explained fully in the next chapter.

If you are very clear about what you want the trainee to do, how they should do it and why, you will be in a very good position to explain to the trainee in an unscripted and natural fashion and according to the trainee's immediate needs. Apart from preparing the information that you will need to explain and guide what the trainee does, there are several other areas of the training method that must be prepared in advance:

- *Demonstrations.* For many instructors a demonstration is an important part of the whole process of instruction. A demonstration, however, does not directly help the trainee to do the skill. Instead, it provides a very indirect overview of the skill to be developed. The overview can be very narrow, for example covering just one small aspect of the task, or it can be very broad. Narrow demonstrations are usually designed to help the trainee's understanding in some very specific way, perhaps by showing how a particular part of the task should be performed. We will call this form of demonstration an explanation because its purpose is to explain how the task should be performed. A very broad demonstration has other uses – take, for example, a demonstration for a group of prospective trainee firefighters. They think they want to be firefighters, but like most of us they probably do not know what is involved. Putting on a demonstration has a use for the firecrew as well as for the new recruits – they get to drill their various skills. So, the new recruits stand in an interested group watching the smoke billow from the windows on the top deck of the training tower. Along comes the appliance with lights and siren. The firecrew climb out with well-practised ease and efficiency. Each one has a job and knows exactly what to do. Some run out hoses and begin to play jets of water on the tower, others quickly don breathing apparatus and rush into the building. From the top of the building they carry out 'casualties' in a variety of ways. When it is all over it comes as a surprise to realize they have to pack all the equipment up again. The demonstration leaves a very clear impression that the job is both physical, dangerous and totally dependent on close teamwork. But that is not all. Over in the far corner of the yard is a motorway pile-up, cars and blood-stained dummies (or even hideously real 'casualties' if the Red Cross is joining the demonstration). A second firecrew pull up and begin to free the injured using a range of specialist equipment. It is only too apparent that the firefighter has some unpleasant times at road traffic accidents. By the end of the demonstration the new recruits have a graphic and very memorable overview of the firefighter's task. This broad demonstration, like most demonstrations, has not helped the observers to do the firefighter job. What it has done is to give them an overview of what they will be asked to do and what is expected of them if they decide to train for that job. They can now start their practice with a mental picture of what is involved. In addition, the knowledge of the task has removed the fear of the unknown. For many trainees it is the lack of knowledge about what will be expected of them that produces the anxiety and worry. A good-quality demonstration helps them to relax, gives them an overview of what is expected and helps them to feel 'I'll be able to do that too.' A poor-quality demonstration tends to make the trainee feel that they will never be able to do the task.

- *Explanations.* An explanation differs from a demonstration in that it is intended to convey much more specific information. An explanation is particularly intended to show the trainee *what* must be done and *how* it must be done. For example, a part of a task may demand that hand position is changed in a particular fashion at a particular stage of the process. Most people would, without thinking, arrange to show the trainee the task being performed so that the changes in hand position can be observed in their natural state. Of itself that would not be very useful because unless the instructor told the trainee what to look for, maybe showing the detail on a very slow-motion performance of the task, the trainee would not know what to look for. There would be a very good chance that the trainee would miss those aspects of the task they were intended to see. That does not matter for a demonstration that was meant to provide an overview of the whole task, but it is not much good in an explanation of the task. At the end of an explanation the trainee should be able to describe to you what to do and how to do it and the *explanation is not complete until the trainee can do that.* The explanations you give to the trainee have to be prepared in advance. The aspects of the task requiring explanation have to be identified, they will have to be explained to the trainee in advance of the performance, the performance must be arranged and, as the performance occurs, you will have to provide a commentary to help the trainee understand what they are seeing or doing. Over the course of the instruction there will be more explanations, on the whole, than there will be demonstrations – that is because the demonstration is providing an overview rather than detailed information. The explanation provides detailed information about particular aspects of the task.

- *Training objectives.* Training and instructing are very similar to a journey. At the end of the journey is a destination – in this case a skilled trainee. There are many routes to that destination and the practice conditions you design are the routes that you, as the guide, have chosen. On the skill journey your role is very like that of a tour guide and, like a tour guide, you will have to find the way. After all, the trainee does not know where they are going or they would not need you to help, would they? It makes good sense, then, for you to have some idea of key landmarks along the route that you can use to measure your progress together. Those landmarks are the training objectives. There are two kinds of training objective. There are objectives you can use at the end of training to find out if the trainee is fully skilled; those are the task performance criteria. There are objectives you can use to measure the trainee's progress in training; these act as stepping stones to the final result. Some books and training courses are based entirely on setting performance objectives in training, both to assess the individual's skills and knowledge and to guide training focus. Some suggestions for further reading are included at the end of the chapter for you to explore further if you wish.

We have now finished our outline of the points you will need to prepare, or at least think about, in advance of the instruction. Much of this pre-instruction detail is explained very well in many training-related books. What is of most interest to us in this book, though, is how to instruct. As we have noted before, few books or articles explain how to do the instruction that follows the preparation. We will now turn to instruction. Bear in mind that however detailed a description we may be able to provide here, it will not be the same as actually doing it. We have the problem that we must talk about something that is an activity. I hope the description of instruction in the next chapter will help you to develop your instructional practice or confirm that what you do already is sound.

Further reading

Task analysis

Annett, J., Duncan, K.D., Stammers, R.B. and Gray, M.J. (1971), *Task Analysis*, Department of Employment, Training Information Paper 6, London: HMSO.

Davies, I.K. (1971), *The Management of Learning*, London: McGraw-Hill.

Patrick, J. (1991), 'Types of Analysis for Training', in Morrison, J.E. (ed.), *Training for Performance, Principles of applied human learning*, Chichester: John Wiley and Sons.

Patrick, J. (1992), *Training: Research and Practice*, London: Academic Press.

Romiszowski, A.J. (1981), *Designing Instructional Systems, Decision making in course planning and curriculum design*, London: Kogan Page.

Analysing thinking skills

Coscarelli, W. (1978), 'Algorithmisation in Instruction', *Educational Technology*, **2**, February, 18–21.

Kopstein, F. (ed.) (1977), 'What is Algorithmisation of Instruction?', *Educational Technology*, **10**, special edition, October.

Landa, L.N. (1982), 'Interview with L. Landa: The Improvement of Instruction, Learning and Performance', *Educational Technology*, Part 1, October, 7–12; Part 2, November, 7–14.

Landa, L.N. (1983), 'The Algo-Heuristic Theory of Instruction', in Reigeluth, C.M. (ed.), *Instructional Design: Theories and Models*, Hillsdale, NJ: Erlbaum, 163–207.

Landa, L.N. (1987), 'The creation of expert performers without years of conventional experience, the Landamatic Method', *Journal of Management Development*, **6**, (4), 40–52.

Merrill, P.F. (1977), 'Algorithmic organisation in teaching and learning: Literature and research in the USA', *Improving Human Performance Quarterly*, **6**, 93–111.

Mitchell, M.C. (1980), 'The Practicality of Algorithms in Instructional Development', *Journal of Instructional Development*, **4**, (1), 10–16.

Analysing physical skills

National Coaching Foundation (1986), *The Coach at Work*, Coaching Handbook 1, Leeds: National Coaching Foundation,

Seymour, W.D. (1954), *Industrial Training for Manual Operations*, London: Pitman.

Seymour, W.D. (1959), 'Training Operatives in Industry', *Ergonomics*, **2**, (2), 143–7.

Seymour, W.D. (1959), *Operator Training in Industry*, London: Institute of Personnel Management.

Seymour, W.D. (1966), *Industrial Skills*, London: Pitman.

Seymour, W.D. (1968), *Skills Analysis Training*, London: Pitman.

Selecting trainees

Jessup, G. and Jessup, H. (1975), *Selection and Assessment at Work*, London: Methuen.

McComisky, J.G. (1968), 'Selecting Trainees', in *Planning Industrial Training*, London: National Institute of Adult Education, England and Wales, November, 28–37.

Robertson, I.T. and Downs, S. (1979), 'Learning and the prediction of performance: Development of trainability testing in the United Kingdom', *Journal of Applied Psychology*, **64**, 42–50.

—, *Trainability Tests: A Practitioner's Guide* (1981), Cambridge, England: Industrial Training Research Unit Ltd.

Toplis, J., Dulewicz, V. and Fletcher, C. (1991), *Psychological Testing – A Manager's Guide*, 2nd edn, London: Institute of Personnel Management.

Analysing the outcomes needed for successful performance of a task

Training Agency, Employment Department Group, (1988), *The Development of Assessable Standards for National Certification: Guidance Note 1 – A code of practice and a development model*, London: HMSO.

The Training Agency, Employment Department Group, (1988), *The Development of Assessable Standards for National Certification: Guidance Note 2 – Deriving Elements of Competence*, London: HMSO.

The Training Agency, Employment Department Group, (1988), *The Development of Assessable Standards for National Certification: Guidance Note 3 – The definition of competences and performance criteria*, London: HMSO.

The Training Agency, Employment Department Group, (1988), *The Development of Assessable Standards for National Certification: Guidance Note 4 – The characteristics of units of competence*, London: HMSO.

The Training Agency, Employment Department Group, 1988), *The Development of Assessable Standards for National Certification: Guidance Note 7 – Identifying underpinning knowledge and understanding*, London: HMSO.

Ways of passing knowledge on to the trainee

Davies, I.K. (1971), *The Management of Learning*, London: McGraw-Hill.

Harrison, R. (1988), *Training and Development*, London: Institute of Personnel Management.

Rae, L. (1990), *The Skills Of Training*, 2nd edn, Aldershot: Wildwood House Ltd (Gower).

12

Delivering instruction

This chapter is the core of the book. In it we discuss and describe the process of instruction as performed by effective instructors.

One of the problems faced in this and subsequent chapters is that of describing in words something that is very dependent on what happens during the trainee's practice. Although I will try to describe the instruction process as accurately as possible, it will not capture the dynamic detail of the process. If you want to develop your instructional skills to become an effective instructor what you will really need is personal instruction in the process of instruction by a competent instructor. But what is a competent instructor? This chapter should help you decide. Because we are describing *how* effective instructors instruct this should help you to modify what you do (if that is needed, of course) and it will also help you to identify effective instructors by giving you some very concrete suggestions on what to look for. Bear in mind that in this chapter we are trying to describe how instructors instruct, and hence how you should go about instructing. Bear in mind also that you will need to have prepared some aspects of your instruction before you begin to instruct. These have been discussed in the previous chapter.

We will start by exploring some of the more general points about effective instruction and then move on to explore how the basic process of instruction happens when you have access to a trainee. For a variety of reasons not all instructors can be with the trainee as they perform the task. Chapter 17 explains how you can instruct a trainee when you do not have the opportunity to be with them as they perform the task.

Guiding the trainee's actions

We are all familiar with the idea of guiding the trainee in what they do and as they do it. Research has found that guidance is very useful, it helps the trainee to master new tasks. Indeed, the presence of guidance could be said to be the defining characteristic of instruction. But trying to summarize the best use of guidance is a complex problem, partly because there are different ways of guiding a trainee. For example:

- *Verbal guidance.* We give the trainee instructions before they perform the task, or as they perform it. For example, 'When the light flashes, adjust the temperature dial' or 'Use your front foot to start the machine and your back foot to stop it.'
- *Visual guidance.* We use demonstrations and illustrations to show the trainees what to do and when to do it.
- *Physical guidance.* We can either force the trainee to move in certain ways or we can allow the trainee to move freely but restrict the movements they make in some way. A forced response could be, say, a stop built into a machine to prevent movement in certain directions or a harness that limits the range of movements possible. Restricted guidance could be, for example, an instructor holding the trainee's hands as they perform a task so as to restrict the movements they make and to provide an idea of the rhythm necessary to perform the task.

Verbal guidance and visual guidance provide the trainee with knowledge before they attempt the task. Physical guidance provides the trainee with information about the movements necessary as they perform the task. All three forms of guidance are at the same time methods of conveying information and ways of preventing the trainee making errors in what they do. But there are subtle variations possible in the way that we guide the trainee and research has uncovered that how we go about guiding is vitally important to the success of our instruction. So, it is the presence of guidance that means we are instructing (rather than, say, educating) but it is how we guide that determines how effective our instruction is. Before we can describe the process of instruction used by effective instructors we need to understand some of the subtleties of instructional guidance.

Guidance in instruction and the trainee's process of skill development

Chapter 9 outlined the following stages in the trainee's development of a skill. Do not forget that the stages are not crisply defined. Each of these stages blends into the next:

1. The trainee attempts to understand the task and how to perform the task.
2. The trainee tries to do the task, but has to concentrate hard in order to do that. As the trainee performs the task he or she will make many mistakes.
3. The task performance becomes automatic and the trainee does not have to concentrate to perform it.

The presence of these three stages has very important implications for you as you instruct. You will have to guide the trainee in differing ways and vary your instructional activities at each stage of skill development.

Instructing in stage 1 of skill development

In the first stage you will be providing demonstrations and explanations for the trainee. You will have to show the trainee what to do, how to do it and may even have to explain why to help the trainee understand. Although it is easy to spend a very great deal of time and effort on this stage as you instruct, it is important that you do not forget the other two stages – they are the stages at which skill proper begins to develop, so they are the stages where instruction becomes very important. In stage 1 you will be doing a lot of verbal, and possibly visual, guidance. To help the trainee you may be doing physical guidance as the trainee moves into stage 2 of skill development – performing the task.

Instructing in stage 2 of skill development

As the trainee starts to perform the task for the first time you will need to help them both perform the skill and avoid making errors. You will have to observe what the trainee does and how it is done – the trainee will be working too hard to really see and understand what they are doing, so you will have to do it for them. You will, in essence, be acting as the trainee's eyes and ears.

In addition you will be acting as a memory resource for the trainee, trying to reduce the memory load that the trainee has to carry at a time of great mental effort. That means you will be warning the trainee as difficult parts of the task appear and will be prompting the trainee to help them remember what to do and how to do it at that point. You will also be reminding or telling them what to do, because they simply will not remember everything they were told in the demonstrations and explanations.

As well as all this, you will be telling the trainee what it is they are doing that is right. The trainee is in no position to know what is right and what is wrong and, in all probability, they are working too hard to notice. If you tell them what is going well it will boost their confidence and help them to remember what to do next time to be correct.

Finally, you will be correcting errors as soon as possible after they happen. We have discussed the power of the trainee's learning machine in earlier chapters. If the trainee practises wrong methods and procedures they will remember and repeat them. It is important that you make sure the trainee only practises the right methods. Immediate correction is therefore very important – that means you must be with the trainee for most of the time in stage 2 of skill development.

In this stage, then, you will almost certainly be performing physical guidance of some sort until the trainee is able to reproduce the correct movements and patterns without your help. As the trainee begins to perform the task independently there may be a need for continued physical guidance of some sort, but this must reduce so that the trainee can perform freely and does not become dependent on the guidance. As free performance increases you must provide verbal guidance to jog the trainee's memory (you are still helping to reduce the memory load for the trainee) so as to encourage correct performance of the task. You will also be giving verbal guidance to give the trainee information about how they are performing the task – they will probably be concentrating too hard to be able to monitor their own performance and adjust what they do. They will need your verbal help and guidance to do that and they will need your verbal encouragement to keep going.

Instructing in stage 3 of skill development

If you perform your role properly in the previous (second) stage of skill development, the trainee will develop proficiency very quickly. Your role will change as the trainee's proficiency grows. As the trainee's performance improves, you will tend to do less of the prompting and the warning – there is less need because the trainee begins to grasp and remember the key points of each aspect of the task and will begin to anticipate what is going to happen next. As the trainee grasps what is happening the performance of parts of the task start to become automatic and the trainee has to put less effort into remembering what to do. You will spend more time asking the trainee as a way of helping them to remember and less time telling them what to do. You will find you are telling the trainee more and more that they are doing very well (because they are) and their confidence will increase. As the trainee masters the task you must make sure that they have enough opportunity to practise it so that it becomes automatic. You must make sure that you slowly withdraw from the trainee's performance, making fewer and fewer interventions, fewer prompts and guides so the trainee learns to think for themself. In this stage you will be doing less and less guidance of any sort.

You can see from this brief outline that your job as instructor is a demanding one. You have to be able to juggle several balls at once with even one trainee; should you have several trainees to instruct then your help will be spread very thin indeed! It is extremely important that you spend as much of your time as possible with the trainee who is starting stage 2 of the skill development process. It is in stage 2 that skill development begins and it is in this stage that the foundations of later performance development are laid. If you can spend time to make sure the trainee performs just the one, correct method then the trainee will quickly gain some proficiency and you can, if absolutely necessary, spend a little time away from the trainee, although this is not recommended. Research has found that the more trainees an instructor has to deal with the more time it takes the trainees to achieve performance criteria. The research found that each additional trainee in the training school added nearly one week to the training time for each individual trainee.

It is also extremely important to notice that your role changes as the trainee gains skill. What works as an instructional technique in the early stages of skill development is not likely to work in the later stages, and vice versa. Research exploring what made some instructors effective and others ineffective found that it was the inflexibility of instructional technique that led to poor instructing outcomes. An effective instructor almost shares the task with the trainee and, as a result, changes the instruction as the trainee changes and develops.

Finally, the brief descriptions of the stages of skill development show how important it is to use the trainee's skill development as the organizing principle of instruction. If we try to explain what happens in instruction without using the trainee's skill development as a skeleton from which to hang the instructional techniques we quickly find that there is no clear message. Instructional techniques and guidance techniques must be chosen according to the trainee's needs. The trainee's needs change as skill develops and guidance that is right for the early stages of skill development is not necessarily right for the later stages.

Let us expand the descriptions above to look at some aspects of instruction and guidance in more detail. We will discuss each aspect in the sequence we might expect to use it in the instructional process.

Demonstrating and explaining

Demonstrations and explanations provide useful methods of verbal and visual guidance for the first stage of skill development. In the later stages they lose their effectiveness. Unfortunately, for many instructors demonstrations and explanations are what instruction is all about. Demonstrations and explanations are useful only if they are seen as tools to be used in the early stages of skill development. Like any tool they have their proper and improper uses, there are times when they are very useful, times when they are less useful. How should demonstrations be used as effective training tools?

Demonstrations

First we have to understand what demonstrations are useful for. We defined a demonstration earlier as providing an overview of the skill for the trainee. A demonstration is very rich in information, far too much information for the trainee to remember it all. However, that richness gives the trainee an opportunity to see how different parts of the task fit together and their relative place in the whole task. This, coupled with some explanation, enables the trainee to see the importance of different aspects of the whole task and develop some feel for how fast different parts of the task must or should be performed. In that light it makes sense for the demonstrations to come primarily at the start of training when the trainee is lacking that information. Following the demonstration the trainee will be well placed to understand the training tasks. Most research has found that demonstrations becomes less useful in the later stages of training – and that is understandable, a demonstration in the later stages of skill development is probably not telling the trainee anything new.

There is a role for demonstrations in the early to middle stages of skill development. Practising a skill can be very demanding on the trainee and they will almost certainly become very tired. In industry, certainly, there is often a great pressure on the instructor to keep the trainees busy even if they are tired, but this can be counter-productive. A tired trainee may perform in a tired fashion, and such is the power of the learning machine that they will often learn to perform the skill in a tired fashion as a result. It can make more sense to allow the trainee to practise only when they are fresh and able to learn to perform the skill in a fresh manner. So what should you do when they become tired? If there is a knowledge element to learn it can be useful to stop practice on the task and spend some time covering the knowledge element of the task. An alternative to this is to arrange for a demonstration of the next part of the training process – that is particularly useful if the trainee is coming to the end of the present training task and is ready to move on to the next. The demonstration provides an opportunity to rest and an opportunity to start thinking about the next phase of practice.

Finally, although demonstrations are not often useful in the later stages of skill development, there is a form of demonstration that can be extremely powerful for the trainee, especially in the later stages of skill development. The demonstrations we have been talking about so far have been to give the trainee an overview of the task and its requirements. This is not needed in the later stages of developing skill. However, the later stages can be demanding for the trainee in a different way. It is in the later stages that the skill patterns are burned into the trainee's brain. Constant repetitive practice of a skill, whether closed or open, can be wearing for the trainee. The practice is necessary if the skills are to become automatic and refined, but the trainee does need to be encouraged to keep it up. In sport, you can achieve this by entering trainees into competitions but that is not so easy in industry. However, if you have access to video facilities you can provide a demonstration for the trainee based on the trainee's own performance. You should video the trainee in the very early stages of skill development when the trainee's performance is slow and uncertain, then video the trainee when skill is well developed and performance is fairly good. When the trainee is tired or needs to be encouraged to continue practice, a demonstration of her or his progress – a 'before and after' – can be a very positive event. The visible progress in skill acts as a powerful reward and you can build on that by discussing with the trainee where performance can be improved. That discussion leads into the next phase of practice and provides some useful training objectives to work towards. The new performances can also be recorded to provide the basis for future coaching discussions.

Explanations

So far we have talked about demonstrations but what about explanations? We defined an explanation earlier as an event that was intended to show the trainee what to do and how to do it. An explanation is much more specific than a demonstration. Explanations are intended to give the trainee information they can use to help them do what they are supposed to do. If the trainee cannot remember the information then there has been a problem with the explanation. Because the explanation is intended to help the trainee by providing important background information the explanation is finished only when the trainee can describe, repeat or otherwise show they have understood and remembered what you have said to them. This is an important point – many explanations fail because the trainee cannot do something new following the explanation or cannot do something better after the explanation. What can go wrong with explanations and what should you do about it? Here are some of the commonest problems and some ways to tackle them:

- *Problem: the trainee does not listen.* You will have to gain the trainee's attention – asking questions and asking the trainee to explain to you (after you have explained, of course) can be very useful ways of doing that.
- *Problem: you do a one-shot explanation and expect the trainee to remember everything.* You may well have to explain or show the point several times before the trainee grasps everything you are trying to convey. Do not expect the trainee to understand or remember after just one run-through.
- *Problem: you don't vary the explanation.* The aim of the explanation is to get information into the trainee's head. The explanation you start with, the method of explanation and the way you go about it, may not be the best way for that trainee. For example, you may want to explain verbally, but the trainee may grasp information most easily by seeing what happens. You must vary your explanation and use several means of getting the points across. Ineffective instructors stick to one explanation and do not vary what they do.
- *Problem: your explanations may be too long and the trainee's attention wanders.* Paying attention for long periods and to new and possibly complex information is tiring. Most people cannot pay attention for long. You have several options: make your explanations shorter, make the explanations more interesting and stimulating, ask many questions as you explain, use varying means of making the points so the trainee does not lose interest.
- *Problem: you may be giving the trainee too much information to remember.* Remembering complex information is difficult; there is a natural limit for most people beyond which they cannot remember what they see or hear. Try to limit your explanations to the amount of information the trainee can remember and put into practice – that will vary for each trainee. In addition, some methods of explanation are more difficult to remember than others for different people and for different tasks. Many people find visual explanation easier to remember than verbal, a few find verbal explanations easier to remember than visual. For movement tasks, especially when using the hands, explanations using the body senses can be very effective. Body senses are those we use to control how we move about but they are senses we do not pay a great deal of conscious attention to. For example, touch, rhythm, movement itself, can all be very important cues for the trainee to

remember when carrying out a pattern of movement. It is possible to guide the trainee's hands to show how a pattern of movement feels or it is possible to use equipment that forces the trainee to move in certain ways. These are only useful as explanations, though; they are ways of helping the trainee to grasp what must be done in free movement. Too much guidance or restrained movement will hinder the development of the skill as the trainee learns to depend on the guidance rather than his or her own control of movement. In the early stages of skill development explanations should be focused on what the trainee needs to know that will help him or her perform the task. In the later stages of skill development explanations are more useful if they give relevant background information which will help the trainee to perform the task but which is not necessary for the task's performance.

Bibliography

Gershoni, H. (1979), 'An investigation of behaviour changes of subjects learning manual tasks', *Ergonomics*, 22, (11), 1195–1206.

Holding, D.H. (1965), *Principles of Training*, Oxford: Pergamon Press.

Martin, G. and Hrycaiko, D. (1983), 'Effective behavioural coaching: What's it all about?', *Journal of Sports Psychology*, 5, (1), 8–20.

Romiszowski, A.J. (1968), *The Selection and Use of Teaching Aids*, London: Kogan Page.

Rush, D.B. and Ayllon, T. (1984), 'Peer Behavioural Coaching: Soccer', *Journal of Sport Psychology*, 6, 325–34.

13

Talking to trainees

Previous chapters have described what to do and how to do it when instructing. There is another dimension to instruction that is as important – how you talk to the trainee when instructing. This chapter introduces this important aspect of instructional technique.

One of the most important tools that you will use as an instructor is talking with the trainees or, as it is often termed, verbal guidance. Instructors talk to trainees for many reasons: to give them important information, to correct errors, to prevent errors and to help the trainees to think for themselves, to name but a few. Are there ways of doing this which are better than others? Yes. Researchers found that there were very significant differences between the methods used by effective instructors and those who were less effective.

Effective instructors and ineffective instructors tend to start instruction in a similar manner and then they diverge in what they do. Both effective and ineffective instructors talk a lot in the first few hours of training a new trainee. The effective instructors then decrease the amount of talking they do. The ineffective instructors continue to talk a great deal.

Ineffective instructors tend to spend much of their time giving directions and orders to the trainee – in effect, doing the trainee's thinking for them. In contrast, the more effective instructors do less of this, allowing the trainee to learn to think for themselves but monitoring what is happening so that any performance errors can be corrected immediately. We have noted previously that correcting errors is extremely important. Research has found that both effective and ineffective instructors correct errors at about the same rate. They differ, however, in how they go about doing it. In order to describe how to correct errors we have to recall that there are two major classes of skills: doing skills (or movement skills) and thinking skills (see Chapters 6 and 7).

Effective instructors deal with movement skill errors differently from thinking skill errors. Movement skills are very easy to learn for the learning machine – it has had many millions of years of practice at doing this. In contrast, thinking skills are a recent innovation for humans and the learning machine tends to deal with them less easily. They are often learned via the learning skills we acquire as we grow (see Chapters 5 and 6). That suggests that movement skill errors should be corrected immediately or they will be learned and will cause performance problems. It is better if they do not become fixed in the first place. Hence, effective instructors correct movement skill errors immediately. Ineffective instructors may tell the trainee that they are not performing well but fail to explain what to do or fail to correct immediately. (Do not forget that correction involves helping the trainee to do it properly.) Correction is *not* merely pointing out that something is wrong or telling what to do. Correction involves, potentially at least, bringing all of the instructional techniques to bear to help the trainee to perform the task correctly. Effective instructors will do this if necessary; for ineffective instructors a brief verbal explanation or a comment will do for most circumstances.

When the trainee has to learn thinking skills in conjunction with the movement skills (for example, a bus driver has to learn movement skills to control the bus and thinking skills to interpret what other road users are doing, plan what to do in response and modify the plan if necessary – much of driving is a thinking skill) effective instructors tend to let the trainees make decisions and put them into practice. They will delay their error correction until the trainee can see the consequences of their actions and then the instructors will ask questions to help the trainee think through what has happened. If necessary the effective instructor will offer advice and make suggestions, and that is particularly helpful in the early stages of skill development. As skill develops, however, the effective instructors will use careful questioning to help the trainees to reach the correct conclusions and decisions for themselves.

Ineffective instructors do the opposite. As their trainees develop skill in movement the ineffective instructors start to explain in more and more detail about the decisions and thinking that must be done. They talk more than effective instructors and swamp the trainees with information which makes thinking difficult and makes paying attention to the task difficult (and makes paying attention to the instructor difficult too). This has the overall effect of decreasing the amount of participation by the trainee in the training process. Again, we can contrast that with the effective instructors whose questioning and allowing the trainees to perform encourages trainee participation.

How can we recognize participation by the trainee? The trainees of effective instructors answer questions, ask for information, challenge what the instructor has said and may disagree. The trainees of effective instructors have their own minds and they are being encouraged to be active and think for themselves.

Bear in mind that tasks vary and the safety aspects of some tasks make it less likely that trainees will be given their heads to perform and make mistakes. On the other hand, this is so valuable a process that many intrinsically dangerous tasks which also demand high levels of thinking skill are often taught using simulations and practice conditions which allow the trainee to try it in a risk-free environment. You are the only person who can decide how to balance the safety requirements you face and the need to allow the trainee to develop skill by making mistakes and having them corrected, using excellent instructional techniques.

Table 13.1 summarizes this section with some dos (what effective instructors do) and don'ts (what ineffective instructors do) for instructional excellence.

Table 13.1 How effective and ineffective instructors instruct

	Effective instructors	Ineffective instructors
Talking	Give the trainee just the information they need, when they need it Use silence to give the trainee time to absorb information The amount of talking decreases as the trainee gains skill	Talk too much, especially in the early stages of training when the trainee is still trying to understand what to do and how Do not give the trainee time to absorb information Talk more than effective instructors at each stage of skill development Do not allow the trainee to ask questions
Giving orders and directions to the trainees	Give directions and orders to the trainee as needed in the early stages of training but then increasingly allow trainees to perform freely	Give many orders and directions to the trainee, hence they do not allow the trainee to perform freely
Correcting movement skill errors	Early in skill development, observe the trainee's performance and warn the trainee as difficult areas present, prompting them to encourage correct performance Correct movement errors immediately they occur by 'telling' in the early stages of skill development. In the later stages, correct by asking questions	Allow trainees to perform incorrectly before correcting the errors Note there is an error ('That's not right') but fail to explain what and how to do it correctly In the later stages of skill development, tend to explain what to do and why rather than ask questions to correct
Correcting thinking skill errors	Allow trainees to perform freely, but observe closely as they perform to monitor methods used and outputs produced Allow trainees to make mistakes (if safe to do so), delay error correction to allow trainee the opportunity to correct the error. If the trainee fails to notice, ask questions to help the trainee think through the error and its correction	Fail to observe the trainee to monitor the methods used and outputs produced Give orders and directions that prevent free performance of the task, hence denying the trainee the opportunity of taking control Correct errors immediately and tell the trainee what to do, hence denying the trainee the opportunity to notice and correct the error

Table 13.1   continued

Encouraging trainees to think for themselves	Allow trainees to perform freely, but observe closely as they perform	Overload the trainee with information, increasing the chance of the trainee switching off from what is said
	Allow trainees to make mistakes, delay error correction to allow trainee the opportunity to correct the error. If the trainee fails to notice, ask questions to help the trainee think through the error and its correction	Do not encourage questions or challenges
	Encourage the trainee to seek information, ask questions, and challenge the instructor	
	As skill develops, withdraw from the trainee leaving the trainee with more and more responsibility for performing the task	
Swamping the trainee with too much information	At the start of training use the bare minimum of information needed for the performance of the task	Give very detailed information from the start of training
	As skill develops, give the trainee additional supplementary information as needed	Continue to give excess and unnecessary amounts of information as training continues
	Use silence to allow the trainee to absorb and use information at their own pace	Fail to grant the trainee periods of information-free time, hence denying the trainee opportunity to absorb the information at their own pace

Further reading

Flegg, D., Warren, A. and Law, C. (1982), *POISE: Project On Instructor Style and Effectiveness*, Cambridge: Industrial Training Research Unit.

Flegg, D. (1983), 'Developing Instructor Effectiveness – the P.O.I.S.E. approach', *Personnel Management*, May, 38–40.

Newsham, D. and Fisher, J.M. (1972), 'What's in a style?', *Industrial and Commercial Training*, June, 291–5.

Newsham, D. (1976), *Choose an Effective Style*, research papers TR9 and TR11, Cambridge: Industrial Training Research Unit.

14

Helping the trainee to avoid errors

It is important in the early stages of skill development to prevent the trainee making errors in performance – errors may be learned! Error prevention can be achieved partly by carefully designed practice but mostly error prevention is something that you do as the trainee performs. This chapter outlines how to help the trainee avoid making errors.

The point of guidance during instruction is to help the trainee avoid making errors in performance as they practise the new skills. If they make errors there is a danger that those errors will be indelibly recorded by the automatic learning machine. If the trainee can perform the task correctly it becomes easier for them to notice if there is any variation in their performance. This makes it easier for them to correct their own performance errors later in training. So it is very important that you help them to avoid errors. How do you do it?

The first requirement is that you are present as the trainee performs the tasks – you should be present whether the tasks are training practice exercises or the task proper. It is particularly important that you are present in the early stages of skill development as that is the stage when the trainee will make most mistakes. We noted above that visual and verbal guidance give the trainee pre-knowledge about what they are to do. Demonstrations and explanations are obvious examples of how this can be done. Less obvious is the verbal guidance that you can give *as the trainee performs*. This guidance is exceptionally useful in helping the trainee avoid making errors in the early stages of skill development.

At the start of stage 1 of skill development you will carry out your explanations and begin to tell the trainee what to do and how to do it. As soon as the trainee begins to perform the task, stage 2 of skill development begins and you must watch and help them to remember what to do and how to do it. This on-the-job verbal guidance has a technical name: feedforward. You are feeding the trainee information about what is to happen next. You will be telling them, for example, what to look for and how to respond and reminding them of what to do and how to do it. You will be doing this as they perform the task. The aim of feedforward is to help the trainee to avoid making mistakes in performance.

Errors can be demoralizing for the person making them, and in business errors can also be expensive. Neither of these situations is helpful to the coach who wishes to develop someone's skill quickly and efficiently. If errors are being avoided then that means that the person is probably practising only the good methods. This will bring results which will boost morale and will also speed learning because there is more opportunity to practise and hence to learn the correct behaviours.

You can provide feedforward information both as the trainee performs the task (on the job) or prior to the trainee performing the task (off the job). In both you are providing prompts to the learner to help them avoid error. In the early stages of skill development it is most useful to observe the trainee and prompt as they perform. This has the effect of helping the trainee avoid making errors and it helps to reduce the memory load on the trainee – you are acting as a sort of spare memory until the trainee gains enough skill to free up some of their own memory. We will discuss on-the-job feedforward now and leave a discussion of off-the-job feedforward for Chapter 17.

Feedforward on the job

It makes sense to work with the trainee as the trainee performs. If you are not present there is a danger that the trainee will unknowingly change what they do and learn the mistakes. In the early stages when the learner is not very skilled you will need to provide very specific information about what is about to happen and how to react: 'When the light flashes then press both buttons together'; 'If your opponent is moving away follow him, put him under pressure!'; 'You're now coming up to a junction, so check the mirror, signal and move to the centre of the road.'

As the learner gains skill you should continue to warn but provide less information. This will encourage the trainee to organize their own response as they will have to do when fully skilled. As your level of information-giving decreases your level of questioning will tend to increase: 'The light is about to flash so get ready ...'; 'Watch your opponent's stance change!'; 'I want you to turn right at the next junction, so what should you do?'.

As the learner becomes proficient you will need to guide and prompt less and less because there is less and less need to. Prompting like this becomes important when the trainee is practising an open skill, where the skill has to be modified to meet the environment's demands (see Chapter 7). You will need to observe the situation with the trainee's eyes so that you can draw their attention to the right environmental cues and give them the right advice.

As well as guiding to help trainees perform without error, it is possible to guide the trainee by correcting their mistakes. This area is a minefield for the unsuspecting instructor. How you do this is so important that we will discuss it extensively in the next chapter.

15

Correcting trainee errors

As the trainee performs a new skill they will make many mistakes. It is important that those errors are corrected quickly or the trainee may repeat the error and come to learn the incorrect method. As with so much of instruction, there is a useful way to correct errors and a less useful way. This chapter explains how to correct trainee errors so as to build confidence and improve performance.

Feedback

Giving the trainee information after their performance goes by the technical name of feedback. Many people are familiar with this term and to some extent it has entered everyday language. Like many words which enter everyday use the meaning can alter from its original; so we need to discuss what we mean by feedback.

Feedback refers to information which is fed back to someone about something they have done. It occurs after the event and should give the person knowledge of the results they have achieved and/or how the methods that they used contributed towards success or failure. There are many reasons why it is necessary to give feedback. Let us look at two of them.

1. When someone is trying hard to master a complex skill or change their behaviour in certain ways most of their attention is focused on doing the job. In this sort of situation the learner finds it extremely difficult to stand back from what is happening because he or she is so busy trying to do it. Because of this, people are largely unaware of the blocks to greater skill development that can arise. This is why you are so vital to the process. You can act as an external observer to monitor and feed back to the trainee what they are doing. That leaves the trainee free to concentrate on the doing. So, by acting as an external monitor for the trainee, you can speed up the skill development.
2. The feedback can act as a reward. For many years it has been recognized that reward is a very powerful way of fixing and making permanent what-

ever pattern of behaviour is desired. The way in which this is carried out is very important and there are lots of ifs and buts involved, but there is no doubt that feedback as reward is a powerful tool to be used in developing skill. This is discussed in more detail below.

These reasons for giving feedback are focused on the trainee performing the task and you giving them immediate feedback as they perform. Feedback can also be given in the longer term to review progress. As a person practises it can be very difficult for them to notice a gradual improvement. Feedback which takes a longer-term review approach can demonstrate to the person that progress is being made. This long-term feedback can be very useful in maintaining the trainee's desire to continue training.

We spoke above of using feedback as a reward. This is a positive use of feedback. It is also possible to use a negative feedback style (or punishment). Before we look at the impact of positive (reward) and negative (punishment) styles let us have some examples of each. Tick the appropriate box in Exercise 1 when you have identified whether the example is positive or negative:

EXERCISE 1

	Positive?	Negative?
1. 'You did that exactly as we agreed, well done'		
2. 'That could have been better, couldn't it?'		
3. 'Now, what went wrong there?'		
4. 'What do you think went well that time?'		
5. 'Excellent! Well done'		
6. 'Hmm'		
7. 'Oh no! Why did you let that happen?'		
8. 'Yes that's right, do it like that again'		
9. 'That's not too bad, not bad at all'		

Some of these feedback comments in Exercise 1 are ambiguous in their tone, for example, 6 and 9. Number 6 says nothing at all, so why say it? What sort of an effect would that have on a trainee who has been trying hard and then looks to you for comment? It is most likely to deflate rather than boost the trainee. That said, the context is important. Suppose a trainee has argued strongly that she could not do, say, a particular twisting dive but you have persuaded her to try anyway. She tries it and performs a good dive. As she climbs from the pool, she catches your eye and you promptly respond with comment 6: 'Hmm'. In that context it is more likely to be taken as a friendly or positive comment.

Number 6 is an example of a comment that it is better to avoid unless the trainee knows you very well and is very skilled. In the early stages of skill development the trainee needs strong and definite feedback. Comment 9 is an example of a common phrase used by instructors. It is meant to be positive but somehow the positive comment has been twisted into very grudging praise. It is easy to inadvertently damn the trainee's efforts by faint praise. Be definite in your praise (for example, 1, 5, 8) and avoid comments like number 9. Some of the comments are negative in tone – numbers 2, 3, and 7 – these are better avoided. Not only do they undermine the trainee, as we will show below, but they do not really help. Do not forget that the trainee needs to know what they are doing well so they can repeat what they have just done. Useful feedback comes from comments such as those in numbers 1, 4, 5 and 8. Let us now look at the different ways of giving feedback so that we can identify what are the best methods to use and what methods should be avoided.

Feedback styles

We have just seen that it is possible to give feedback to trainees in different ways and with differing emphases. Not surprisingly an individual instructor comes to use one style more often than other styles of feedback. Some may use strongly positive feedback often, others may use weak negative feedback more often. If we take a step back we find that there are just four basic styles of feedback. I will describe them and then suggest which of these styles is most effective in helping the trainee to improve.

Look at example number 5 in Exercise 1. It is praise, but it is general praise. It says nothing about what the trainee has done that is good; it is not factual. Now have a look at example number 1. There the instructor is doing more than just praising the trainee; there is a degree of fact involved – the trainee did it just as had been agreed. So we can distinguish between feedback that is factual and feedback that is not factual. Let us call the factual feedback objective and the non-factual feedback subjective.

Objective feedback deals with the facts of what has occurred. Strictly speaking, in objective or factual feedback several observers should be able to see the same observable events that the trainee has performed. Subjective feedback is the opinion of the observer. In feedback, subjective opinions are often easy to spot as they reveal the feelings of the instructor.

As a general guide it can help to put yourself in the position of the trainee receiving the feedback. If the feedback makes the trainee feel good or bad it was subjective, especially if there is no guidance on how to correct the performance or no factual evidence. If the feedback discusses how to correct or exactly why what the trainee did was correct, or if it contains factual information, it was probably objective. Try Exercise 2.

EXERCISE 2

	Objective?	Subjective?
1. 'You did that exactly as we agreed, well done'		
2. 'That wasn't too good, was it?'		
3. 'No, no, no! That's not right'		
4. 'I think that went well that time'		
5. 'Excellent! Well done'		
6. 'Over the last two weeks you've lost six sales out of twenty'		
7. 'Over the last two weeks you've gained fourteen sales out of twenty'		
8. 'Yes that was good, do it exactly like that again'		

The objective feedback comments are 1, 6, 7 and 8. Although number 8 does not contain detailed information it does refer to something that both the instructor and the trainee are likely to understand as detailed and factual. The other comments are more subjective, containing little factual information or failing to refer to specific details that both instructor and trainee can see and understand.

In addition to the objective–subjective split between feedback information, it is also possible to make positive and negative comments. For example, comments numbers 2 and 3 in Exercise 2 above are negative; they focus on what has gone wrong. But they also contain little factual information, so they are subjective in nature as well – subjective–negative feedback. Comments 4 and 5 are also subjective but they are positive in nature. It is easy to think of subjective feedback as being either positive or negative – the feeling that results for the trainee on the receiving end is either pleasure or pain. However, objective feedback can be positive or negative as well. Look at comments 6 and 7 above. They both describe the same situation but one looks at it from a negative viewpoint and the other from a positive viewpoint.

In our culture there is a strong bias towards looking at a trainee's performance from a problem or difficulty orientation, hence even objective feedback is likely to be given in the form of negative comments. It does not have to be and it is more effective if it is not – positive feedback is very effective at boosting confidence and trainee motivation, negative feedback has the opposite effect. Positive, objective feedback also helps the trainee to know what is going well so they can try to repeat what they have just done.

Let us combine the differing feedback styles into a table format so we can see how they compare – Figure 15.1 shows the four feedback styles.

We now have four feedback styles available for you to use. The subjective styles give general, non-specific information to the trainee. This feedback cannot help the trainee to change performance because no information about what is right or wrong has been given to them. But saying to someone 'Excellent! Really well done' can be a powerful reward which boosts confidence. Being negative is just as powerful but it destroys the trainee's confidence and willingness to try, as we shall see later. Objective, or more factual, feedback proves to the trainee that the reward is justified. It also helps the trainee to know what went well and why.

If the trainee is to avoid making errors and build on what is being done correctly you must give them factual feedback. There are two forms of factual feedback, a positive and a negative form. Both are powerful but only one is constructive and that is the positive form. Positive feedback concentrates on what the trainee has done which is correct or desirable. Which of these four styles of feedback are used most commonly and which are of most use to you?

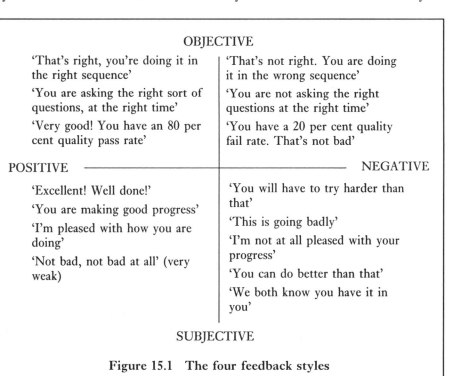

OBJECTIVE

POSITIVE	NEGATIVE
'That's right, you're doing it in the right sequence'	'That's not right. You are doing it in the wrong sequence'
'You are asking the right sort of questions, at the right time'	'You are not asking the right questions at the right time'
'Very good! You have an 80 per cent quality pass rate'	'You have a 20 per cent quality fail rate. That's not bad'
'Excellent! Well done!'	'You will have to try harder than that'
'You are making good progress'	'This is going badly'
'I'm pleased with how you are doing'	'I'm not at all pleased with your progress'
'Not bad, not bad at all' (very weak)	'You can do better than that'
	'We both know you have it in you'

SUBJECTIVE

Figure 15.1   The four feedback styles

Feedback styles commonly used in instruction

Most of us are trained in both school and work situations to focus on problems and identify the causes of problems. This approach is used, innocently enough perhaps, to ensure that the problems are put right. However, a problem-centred approach has two major outcomes which are less desirable. First, it becomes very easy to allocate blame as a part of finding the cause of the problem (for example, 'Who did it this way and why?'); second, the extent of the problem is often emphasized in order to make the problem a high priority for solution (for example, 'It's really terrible', or 'The whole lot is useless'). Unfortunately these become habits and when it comes to giving feedback these habits come to the fore. The result is that many instructors inadvertently use a feedback style which falls into the negative side and often into the negative–subjective box alone. We can all think of teachers or sports coaches we have had who often use that form of negative, subjective feedback.

The other common feedback style is based on trying to be supportive to the trainee – using a positive but subjective style. It can be pleasant to be on the receiving end of this positive–subjective feedback, but after a while the trainees tend to ignore or discount it. Instructors who use the style indiscriminately sometimes come to be known as 'mother hens'. The problem with it is that it gives the trainee little specific information about what they have done well, gradually becoming background noise, pleasant noise no doubt, but in the background nevertheless.

What are the most effective styles?

A great deal of research in the area of skill development has shown that the feedback styles which are most effective are the positive styles. The trainee needs to know what they are doing well so that they can continue to do it that way in future (positive–objective feedback). If you can combine this useful information with a reward (positive–subjective feedback) the message is emphasized and the trainee's commitment and enthusiasm is increased.

Although the negative–objective feedback style has its place it must be used with caution. Its major use would be in the situation where the trainee is doing something unsafe or very dangerously wrong. An objective discussion of this may help the trainee to avoid the difficulty in future. Because an objective discussion is relatively constructive and less threatening than general negative comments the trainee's morale is not likely to be damaged. This will be especially true if the negative–objective feedback can be combined with positive feedback at the same time.

The negative–subjective style is of little use because it merely punishes without giving useful information which the trainee can use to help them improve in future. It should be avoided.

Think very carefully, now: what is the style that you use most? Do you need to change how you give feedback? Here is a case study to illustrate what could happen if you do change your approach. Jean was an instructor in a textile factory. She attended an instructing course where she was told about the four feedback styles. She went away with a firm resolve to use the positive–objective style with her trainees. When she was followed up some weeks later she was very definite about how useful that style had been for her: 'I used to have trouble with absenteeism, but now I can't stop them at the end of the day. They won't go home! I can't supply them with enough work – they are doing really good quality work.' Because she was telling the trainees they were doing well (positive–subjective feedback) and giving proof that they were doing well at the same time (positive–objective feedback) they could not ignore what she said. They were so excited at being competent that they did not want to stop.

Many books on instruction recommend you praise the trainee when they do something well. That has a very powerful effect – or, to be more precise, it has several powerful effects: it boosts their confidence by providing success-based information (as the research above showed) and it also helps the trainee to know when they are doing something correctly so they can repeat it. Using praise is very important as an instructional technique, so let us try to understand the role of praise in instruction.

Why does praise work?

There are two main explanations why praise works. Which explanation you choose to accept is up to you. The first explanation involves the idea of reward and comes from a school of psychology that has been very influential in the past, behavioural psychology. The main idea here is that if certain actions are rewarded in some way creatures (including humans) will tend to increase the number of times they perform those actions. What counts as a reward varies from food to, in humans, a smile and a friendly word. Using this approach it is possible to train animals to act in very bizarre ways; it is often used to train animals for film parts, for example. It is a very powerful way of shaping behaviour in animals and in some human situations. Whether it works in training is a point to debate and you must decide if you want to use this as a way of instructing. Its application to instruction would be as follows: as the trainee performs you should watch their performance carefully. When the trainee performs an action correctly, immediately reward that correct performance to increase the chance of that correct performance occurring again. What a reward is for a particular trainee may vary, of course. For some, a 'well done' may be rewarding; for others, a pat on the back or a public recognition of the achievement may be enough. And there lies the real difficulty: what exactly is a reward? When we train a purposely starved animal it is easy to see that the animal will want to work for more food by repeating actions that produce the rewarding food. But will humans act in the same way? In carefully controlled circumstances (like using purpose-starved trainees) they probably will, but day-to-day training may not be one of those circumstances. The whole idea of reward in humans is fraught with complications of this sort and the crude simplifications used in many older training articles and books do not seem to work very well. For this reason I will not recommend this way of explaining why praise works. Instead I will suggest a second, alternative explanation which seems to work well for most instructors.

The alternative explanation for the effect of praise is to think of it as information that the trainee needs. A trainee is, by definition, ignorant. They are working very hard, concentrating on trying to perform complex and new actions. They are experiencing a whole new world of sensation and activity and simply do not know whether what they are doing is right or wrong. If as they perform you tell them what they are doing right, they can make a conscious effort to remember that and repeat that pattern of movement and feeling. If you do not tell them when what they do is correct they will not know which methods of moving to repeat. They will not be able to remember how it felt to do it that way and so they cannot monitor what they do the next time they do it. So, by praising them and telling them when they are performing correctly you are giving the trainee important information that they need in order to perform correctly a second time. This explanation is useful in that it suggests that the more specific the information you give the trainee the better. General praise ('That's very good, well done') may have a slight effect but more specific praise has a more powerful effect ('That part of the movement was just at the right speed, well done. Try to do it at that speed again next time').

Boosting the trainee's confidence

The above section discussed giving feedback to the trainee. What about dealing with the trainee's errors? How do you go about drawing the trainee's attention to errors and correcting them? If you do it badly, it could destroy the trainee's confidence and seriously slow the trainee's rate of skill development, so it is important that you know how to deal with trainee errors effectively. There is a research study that is particularly useful to illustrate some of the pitfalls involved in how you correct the trainee's errors.

In the research several groups of trainees were given a simple, repetitive movement task to perform. One group was consistently told they were performing the task better than average, one group was consistently told they were performing worse than average, a third group was told they were doing better or worse at random as they performed, and the fourth group was not told how they were performing at all. What results came from the study?

First, the nature of the information the trainee received influenced how they perceived themselves. The group who had been told they were doing badly came to believe they had less ability to perform the task than did most other people. In contrast, the group who had been told they were doing better than average came to believe they had more ability than most people. In this way the emphasis you place on the trainee's errors can alter the trainee's belief in themselves. Trainees who begin to perceive themselves as having no ability may give up trying, whereas those who believe they have more ability may persevere in training. In this study the trainees who had received no feedback or who received randomized success–failure feedback did not differ in their self-belief from the group who had been told they were performing better than average. This shows that it is the negative feedback that is destructive rather than the success feedback that builds the trainee's self-belief. The lesson is that errors must be dealt with in a way that avoids comparing the trainee un-favourably with other trainees. We will discuss how to do that in the next section.

The second lesson from this study concerns the way the trainees came to view the task – remember, they were all performing the same task. The group who had received positive feedback came to believe that their ability and the effort they put into the task were responsible for the success they were told they were experiencing. They felt the task's difficulty was not important in how well they were doing. As they continued to be told that they were successful they continued to increase their belief that they had great ability and they perceived the task to be increasingly easy to perform and requiring increasingly less effort. In contrast the group who had consistently been told they were performing worse than average felt the task was difficult. As they continued to receive failure feedback they increased their perceptions of the task's difficulty and of the effort needed to do the task. This suggests that if you emphasize to trainees that they are not doing very well they will begin to perceive the task as being difficult and requiring more and more effort to perform. The trainees may well give up attempting to perform the task. Trainees come to believe that if they succeed continually they personally are responsible due to their ability to do the task. If they see that they fail often they come to believe it is the task that is too difficult to perform. The random and no feedback groups did not differ from the success feedback group so again we can see the destructive effect on the trainee of negative information.

A final point from this research study. The four groups did not differ in their actual performance of the task, but were all equally proficient, so we can be sure that it was the feedback they received that produced the differing focus of self-belief between the groups.

What are the implications for you? How should you go about correcting trainee errors to obtain the best outcome?

Giving effective feedback

Although the theory behind feedback in instruction is relatively straight-forward, doing it can be confusing at first. You will need to be able to habit-ually look for the positives in what the trainee is doing. How can you go about practising giving effective feedback? One strategy which you can practise easily is this:

1. Watch the trainee carefully and say something supportive whenever possible.
2. Then say, 'Because ...'.
3. Then give positive factual feedback to explain what it was that the trainee did to deserve the positive feedback.

This is particularly useful in the early stages of skill development when the trainee needs to feel that they are competent and making progress, so in the early stages of training as the trainee begins to develop skill try to give feedback such as: 'That went really well – because you explained to the client what you were going to do and why. He was with you all the way'; 'I think you should be very pleased with your progress: because you were able to make benefit statements to every one of the client's expressed needs. I'm sure that got you the sale'; 'You did well in that tackle: because you kept your head down as we agreed you should and it really made a difference to the power you put in.'

Let us now add to that by thinking about the trainee's future performance. You want the trainee to remember what they are doing correctly, so it is possible to emphasize that and look to future performance at the same time. You can start this process by reinforcing what has been done correctly and giving the trainee some feedforward to the next performance. For example: 'That's the idea: because you were moving about all the time your opponent was struggling to keep track of what was happening. Do it like that again'; 'That swing was better because you stayed relaxed as you did it. Try that again now – remember to keep relaxed'; 'You seem to be getting the hang of these selling techniques: because your contract rate has gone from 25 per cent to 40 per cent in just one week. Keep doing it like that and let's see what happens next week.'

As the trainee's skill develops the emphasis in the feedback will change. In the early stages of skill development you have been focusing on what the trainee is doing correctly and you are helping to reinforce that correct performance by using immediate performance feedback and positive support. That not only builds correct performance, it also boosts the trainee's confidence in their own ability. In the later stages of skill development you will need to focus more on those areas of poor performance to help the trainee overcome any weakness in those areas. As with any performance feedback there is a useful way to do it and a host of less useful ways. The basic approach is to use positive feedback, for example: 'You are doing well, you have a 95 per cent acceptance rate for your unit production. We now have to tackle the remaining 5 per cent that are rejects. Most of those rejects are due to the way you tend to hold the fabric too tightly, so what we will do to put it right is ...'; 'Your techniques and speed are very good but you have a tendency to stand in one place too long. We need to get you moving around more so your opponent can't settle. Here's what we will do ...'; 'You are driving around in traffic very well now. I did notice that your reversing was a bit erratic though, especially on sharp bends. I know what you are doing wrong and how we can put it right, so in the next lesson ... .' All these examples emphasize that the trainee is making good progress and emphasize working to improve areas of weakness and working jointly to achieve that. Although the instructors explain what was going wrong in past performances it is explained in the context of knowing how to put it right. The feedback is also looking to future improvements rather than dwelling on what went wrong in the past. This sort of feedback pattern is well accepted by trainees and helps them to develop their performance to perfection without undermining their self-confidence or leaving them with the feeling that they must do it for themselves.

Summary

The discussion on guidance has been rather long and involved, and has spread over Chapters 12–15. That is because it is so important. It is not enough to prepare and demonstrate and explain to trainees. You also have to be working with them to help them perform, guide what they do, help them avoid mistakes and reinforce what they do that is right. In fact that is what instruction is about. You have to watch the trainee carefully, jog their memory and help them to avoid errors. We called that process feedforward. You also have to review their progress with them, both as they perform ('That's the way, well done!') and afterwards when they are resting. We called that process feedback, and it is something we are all familiar with. But there are effective and ineffective ways of giving feedback. For most purposes a positive style with objective and subjective information is the best approach to use. We have also seen that how you involve yourself with the trainee is important. As the trainee's skill develops you must act differently. In the early stages of skill development you will be giving the trainee information, making suggestions, giving them orders and helping them remember it. In the later stages you will be jogging their memory and asking questions. Eventually you will be withdrawing from the trainee to allow them to practise their skills on their own and without depending on you to make their decisions for them.

Now that we have discussed the instructional process in detail, let us put the detail together and summarize the effective instruction process.

Bibliography

Allison, M.G. and Ayllon, T. (1980), 'Behavioural coaching in the development of skills in football, gymnastics and tennis', *Journal of Applied Behaviour Analysis*, 13, (2), 297–314.

Donahue, J.A., Gillis, J.H. and King, K. (1980), 'Behavioural Modification in Sport and Physical Education: a review', *Journal of Sport Psychology*, 2, 511–22.

McCaughan, L. (1977), 'Attributions induced by four feedback conditions', *New Zealand Psychologist*, 6, 146–56.

Martin, G. and Hrycaiko, D. (1983), 'Effective behavioural coaching: What's it all about?', *Journal of Sports Psychology*, 5, (1), 8–20.

Rush, D.B. and Ayllon, T. (1984), 'Peer Behavioural Coaching: Soccer', *Journal of Sport Psychology*, 6, 325–34.

Singer, R.N. (1977), 'To err or not to err: A question for the instruction of psychomotor skills', *Review of Educational Research*, 47, (3), 479–98.

16

Instructing when you can intervene

Ideally you should be with the trainee as they perform their task. This chapter assumes that you will be and summarizes the instruction process. Chapter 17 summarizes what you must do if you cannot be with the trainee as they perform the task.

Let us start this chapter with a restatement of our approach to instruction: instruction is about changing what trainees do. Part of that process may involve passing knowledge to the trainee but the biggest part of effective instruction is to help the trainee do new things and do them well. In this chapter I will describe how to help the trainee develop their skill and try to create a pattern or a map that you can use to navigate your way around effective instruction. Figures 16.1 and 16.2 summarize the instructional process and should be used in conjunction with the discussions elsewhere in this book which will expand the brief points made in them.

The first point to make about effective instructing is that it is preferable for you to be with the trainee as they perform. This is absolutely necessary when the trainee is developing skill in a movement-based task and it is very necessary in the early stages of skill practice for higher-order skills (where the trainee is learning to respond to unpredictable events). If you are not with the trainee in the early stages they will have difficulty identifying what to respond to and how to respond.

The instructional process begins with preparation. You will prepare your understanding of the task details so that you can help the trainee to perform the task correctly and safely. You will need to prepare a sequence of practice exercises which the trainee can use to develop aspects of the whole skill, before trying to perform the whole task. Each of the practice exercises will have a correct method associated with its performance as well as a range of performance criteria, necessary equipment and so on. You will need to prepare all these resources before beginning the instruction with the trainee. You may need to give some thought to the trainee attributes and abilities that may be necessary before the task can be performed (it may be necessary to select trainees carefully before training can begin).

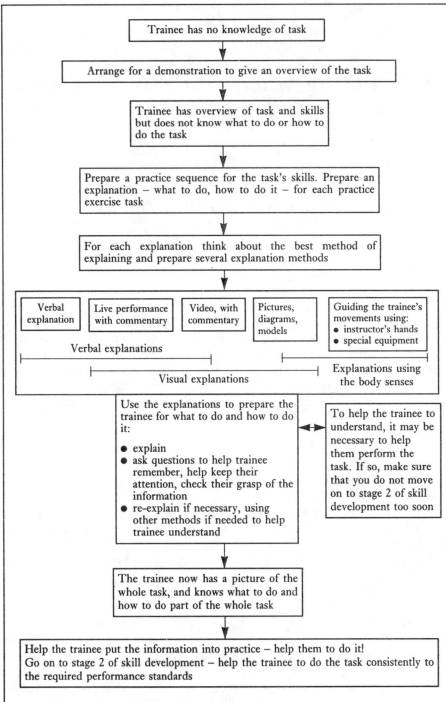

Figure 16.1   Demonstration and explanation

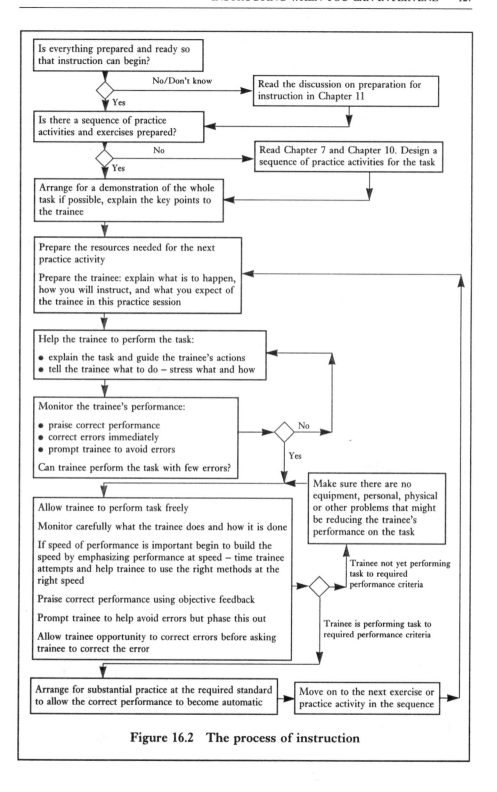

Figure 16.2   The process of instruction

The trainee's skill development begins with a demonstration of the task to be performed. This gives the trainee an overview of what is involved. It may be necessary to explain some of the key points of the task to make sure the trainee understands these before skill development proper begins.

When the trainee has a grasp of the task it is time to begin the skill development process. You will select the first of the practice activities and get everything ready. You will prepare the trainee by explaining what will happen and how the training will proceed. You will then explain how to perform the first activity; because trainees have difficulty remembering a lot of information this explanation may be broken into small parts and combined with guidance on the task itself.

You will help the trainee to perform the task – you will guide their actions either by physically guiding their movements or by showing or modelling out loud the thinking processes to be used. As the trainee attempts to do the task they will make many mistakes. You must correct their errors immediately, praise them for correct performance, explain why the performance was correct and help them to remember what to do by prompting them and telling them.

As the process continues the trainee will come to perform the task with fewer and fewer errors. That is because you are there to prevent and correct errors, so the trainee will only ever practise the right methods and procedures. As errors reduce and performance becomes more confident you should introduce speed emphasis if that is required. The emphasis on speed will produce more mistakes in performance which you must correct as described above. As the trainee performs, monitor the speed and accuracy of their performance and use this to provide positive–objective feedback to the trainee. This will boost the trainee's confidence and encourage them to continue practising. In this stage the trainee will feel tired very quickly. Try to avoid having the trainee practise when tired – they will make more mistakes and make slower progress. Give them rests, and in the rest periods arrange to cover any necessary knowledge areas, then return to the practice.

As the trainee's performance develops you will give the trainee fewer orders and directions. You will allow the trainee to perform freely and give them the opportunity to correct their own errors before prompting them to correct. You will ask the trainee more questions to encourage their own thinking. When they have achieved the performance criteria necessary for this activity (the correct speed, say, and the correct accuracy) that will be the first time that the trainee has achieved the necessary performance criteria. At this point the trainee will begin the process of memorizing the correct performance. You must help that process by arranging for substantial practice on the task. This will help the trainee to make the correct performance automatic and easy to reproduce when needed. At this stage you will be withdrawing from the instructional situation to encourage the trainee to perform independently. When the trainee has mastered the task it is time to move on to the next practice activity and repeat the instructional process.

That is the basic instructional process for helping trainees to do new skills. In some cases it is not possible for you to be with the trainee as they perform the task, so we need to see how the instructional process can be modified so as to continue to be of use to the trainee. The next chapter describes the process of instruction when you cannot be with the trainee as they perform the task.

Further reading

Flegg, D., Warren, A. and Law, C. (1982), *POISE: Project On Instructor Style and Effectiveness*, Cambridge: Industrial Training Research Unit Ltd.

Flegg, D. (1983), 'Developing Instructor Effectiveness – the P.O.I.S.E approach', *Personnel Management*, May, 38–40.

Newsham, D.B. and Fisher, J.M. (1972), *What's in a Style? Measuring the effectiveness of instruction*, ITRU research paper TR3, Cambridge: Industrial Training Research Unit.

Newsham, D.B. (1977), *Choose an effective style II, Developing a course for instructors the Philip's way*, ITRU publication TR11, Cambridge: Industrial Training Research Unit.

Winfield, I. (1988), *Learning to teach practical skills – a self-instruction guide*, 2nd edn, London: Kogan Page.

17

Instructing when you cannot intervene

The essence of effective instruction is to be with the trainee as they perform the task so that you can guide, monitor and correct. Unfortunately it is not always possible to be with the trainee all the time but that does not mean you cannot be effective. This chapter explains how to be an effective instructor even if your trainee has to perform the task when you cannot be present.

With tasks which are closed in nature (see Chapter 7) and also movement tasks it is impossible to instruct effectively if you do not or cannot intervene to help the trainee avoid making errors or to correct performance errors. Why that is should be obvious from the points I have made in previous chapters. With some movement tasks it is simply that it would be downright dangerous were you not present but in general, in the absence of an instructional control, there is just too much room for mistakes in performance and if the trainee performs incorrectly they will learn those mistakes as permanent features of the task.

But with some tasks, mostly open tasks (that is, tasks where actions have to be matched to a particular environmental situation – see Chapter 7) where there is no element of danger involved, it is possible to instruct even when you cannot intervene as the trainee performs. For example, a trainee salesperson goes to visit a client with the aim of performing a real sales call to obtain a sale. It might well be permissible for the trainer to go along as well, maybe even sit in the meeting, but it would undermine the trainee's credibility in a real sales meeting were he to introduce his colleague as his instructor. A similar problem might be experienced by a trainee physiotherapist: it is necessary to perform the skills on real people but too much instruction in the presence of the patient might reduce the trainee's credibility to the point where the patient objects.

Generally you may have to avoid intervening when the trainee has to perform in a commercial or professional relationship with a third party, so how do you maintain effectiveness in that position? There are four points at which you can instruct even when you cannot intervene as the trainee performs the task in real life.

Developing the task skill

If the task is so sensitive that instructional intervention might upset the outcome it seems reasonable to assume that initial skill practice off the job would be a useful approach. How can you go about developing the skills? Many of the sensitive tasks are open tasks where the environment determines the necessary actions. In addition they are tasks where decision making and thinking are likely to be the main element – for example, chairing a meeting, conducting a patient assessment, making a sales call and making a presentation to a large audience are examples where instructional intervention on the job is inappropriate.

As Chapter 7 has shown, it is important that you are certain the trainee is able to perform the basic skills before you go on to arrange task practice. You will need to arrange suitable training to supply the basic skills which are not present. You will also need to supply a real-life simulation that will allow the trainee to practise the application of the skills in an environment where mistakes can be made safely. In other words, if the trainee makes an error there will be no serious outcomes, as there might be were the trainee to practise in the real situation. This simulated practice also allows you to instruct in exactly the way we have described in Chapter 16.

Simulations of the real-life situation are common, particularly in management training. Typical vehicles for this form of safe practice are role-play exercises, although there is a danger with role-play-based training programmes which fail to provide adequate instructional input in that the trainees can have great difficulty in applying the skills they have used in the role-play to the real-life situation. If you use role-play simulation you must make sure that you instruct during the role-play.

Applying the skills on the job

Helping the trainee to acquire the basic skills necessary for the task will be based on your applying the instructional techniques we have discussed above and in other chapters. Helping the trainee to apply the skills on the job may be necessary but that is where you will be unable to intervene. That does not mean you cannot help, however. Here's how.

Preparing for performing the task

You will need to help the trainee think through the task – what must be done, how to do it, what might happen unexpectedly ('What if ...') and how to react to the unexpected. It might be appropriate to have the trainee rehearse some aspects of the task with you prior to performing for real. Rehearsal can be a powerful way of organizing one's thoughts and preparing oneself. In essence you are helping the trainee to avoid error by:

- asking the trainee questions about what has to be done and how it must be done;
- encouraging the trainee to explain what outcomes are expected during the event and afterwards;
- encouraging the trainee to plan ahead to identify events that could be difficult so they can be dealt with successfully;
- asking the trainee to explain what unexpected events could occur and describe how they intend to deal with them;
- providing an opportunity for the trainee to rehearse or role-play immediately before the task's performance.

You will note from this summary that the main vehicle for off-the-job feedforward is questioning rather than telling. Giving trainees information just before they perform is a good way to confuse and overload them. In contrast, asking questions helps them to order their thoughts and prepare in their own way but it is important for you to avoid overdoing it. Too many questions can seem like interrogation and may increase pressure on the trainee. Examples of questions used in off-the-job feedforward are: 'What are you trying to achieve in this meeting?'; 'What are the issues that you need to be clear about before you go in to the meeting?'; 'What particular behaviour do you want to practise in the sales call?'; 'What equipment will you need to use and where is it located?'; 'Tell me a little about the behaviour, when should you use it and how will it help you if you use it?'; 'Give me two examples of the behaviour which you intend to practise in this next sales call'; 'If your customer objects then what does that tell you you are probably doing?'; 'If your customer does object, what will you do?'

Here is a script taken from a physiotherapy training session. The trainee physiotherapist is to work with a patient and the clinical tutor is helping her prepare for the practice:

Physiotherapist tutor:	You've already assessed Mrs Smith, haven't you?
Trainee:	Yes, I assessed her in the department yesterday. She's an in-patient on Ward 6 and she's in for rehabilitation.
Tutor:	Before you did the assessment I asked you to think over what you'd found and decide on a treatment régime for Mrs Smith. What do you feel is Mrs Smith's main problem from your point of view?
Trainee:	She has poor standing balance and is likely to fall.
Tutor:	Why is her balance poor, do you think?
Trainee:	She has reduced pelvic stability due to muscle wasting in her back – she has multiple sclerosis.
Tutor:	Right. So what would you recommend as your treatment aim?
Trainee:	First, to increase her safety, but I'll need to help her improve her balance to do that.

Tutor: Good. What treatment steps are you going to take to help her improve her balance?

Trainee: I've worked out a four-stage plan: first, strengthen her muscles in sitting; second, strengthen her muscles in standing with support; third, assess her for walking aids; and finally, teach her some home-based exercises for strengthening her muscles.

Tutor: That sounds fine. How long do think the first treatment session will take?

Trainee: I've booked her to come down for an hour today, she'll be here in about ten minutes.

Tutor: So we've got time to go through what you intend to do and how. Explain the process you'll use in this first session with Mrs Smith, starting with the sitting exercises.

Trainee: *goes on to explain the technical detail of the exercise programme she intends to use*

Tutor: Why do we start with sitting exercises first?

Trainee: Mostly for safety reasons because of her poor balance, but because she feels secure and well supported she will relax and that will make the guided movements easier for both of us.

Tutor: How will you know when it is time to go on to standing exercises?

Trainee: When she can hold her sitting balance well I think it will be time to go on to standing exercises.

Tutor: OK, how will you know when she has good sitting balance?

Trainee: I'll be able to feel her muscle tone improve and I'll also be able to feel how much control she takes in the guided sitting exercises. When she begins to take control of the movement from me I think she will be ready for the standing exercises – but I won't rush her.

Tutor: That's good, I agree. Tell me what standing exercises you intend in this first session.

Trainee: *goes on to explain the technical detail of the exercise routine she will use*

Tutor: What will you be watching for when you're doing the standing exercises?

Trainee: I'll be checking her ability to move her weight from one foot to the other, and I'll be looking for good posture.

Tutor: What do you mean by good posture?

Trainee: Her pelvis will be tucked in, her knees will be relaxed and her shoulders will be relaxed.

Tutor: What else will you be looking for?

Trainee: I don't want her to get tired, so I'll be looking out for that.

Tutor:	That's right, good. Don't forget to watch her face as well, you don't want her to struggle and you'll see in her face if she is struggling.
Trainee:	That's useful, thanks, I'll remember that. After the standing exercises I'll be assessing her for walking aids.
Tutor:	Fine, I'll be in the treatment room as well with Mr Jones when you're with Mrs Smith. I'll keep an eye out and when you're ready for the assessment I'll watch too and then, if you need any help or advice, you can pop over and ask ...

Notice how the tutor uses questions to help the trainee to prepare for the task ahead. She uses general questions to help the trainee map out what is going to happen and why, for example: 'What treatment steps are you going to take to help her improve her balance?' They also help the trainee to feel in control of what is happening by asking for the trainee's opinions. The tutor can check that at the same time the trainee's knowledge and plans are adequate.

The tutor also uses focused questions to make sure that the trainee is able to perform key areas of the task, for example: 'What will you be watching for when you're doing the standing exercises?' and 'What do you mean by good posture?' This helps the trainee to bring the important information to the front of her mind ready for use and it also reassures the tutor that the trainee knows what to look for.

Finally, notice that the tutor uses the question and answer session to provide some positive feedback to the trainee: 'That's good, I agree' and 'That's right, good.'

Correcting errors when you cannot intervene or be present

The aim of the pre-performance feedforward is to avoid mistakes in performance. However, trainees make mistakes and even when it is not possible for you to intervene as the trainee performs you must make an attempt to analyse what happened and to correct mistakes. One difficulty, of course, is to find out if mistakes occurred. When you cannot be present it is not really adequate to rely solely on the trainee's account of what happened ('Everything went well, thanks!') although sometimes that is all you can do. You will need to think about how you can increase the reliability of the information about what happened. There are three main strategies open to you:

- Attend the meeting, sales call, etc. and watch what happens. In many cases the problem for you will be that intervention is not possible as the trainee performs. That does not mean that you cannot be present to see what happens. It may be necessary to gain the permission of the third party first and a small deception may be necessary (for example, instead of the trainee introducing you as 'my instructor' arrange to have yourself introduced as 'Ms Jones from our training department who has come along to see how we do sales calls'). When you are installed as an observer you can watch the trainee's performance and make notes ready for the debrief to come.

- Set some form of objectives that have to be achieved during the trainee's performance. Occasionally it will not be possible for you to sit in with the trainee. That is not always a difficulty, especially if you can agree with the trainee beforehand some performance targets that have to be met. For example, it might be possible to agree a checklist that the trainee can use to remind them of what to cover in the meeting (the trainee should tick items off as they are covered). It might be possible to use the notes written by the trainee during the meeting to assess, say, what client problems were uncovered and what responses the trainee made (a particularly useful technique in sales training). Having the trainee write a follow-up letter summarizing the main points discussed and agreed can be a useful way for you to find out what was discussed in the meeting. Another possibility is to have the trainee write up a case report to a predetermined formula to help you to assess what the trainee did when you were not present and what information they found out. The checklists, letters and reports will also form a basis for future pre-activity discussion and agreement. So, by jointly selecting particular skill objectives both you and the trainee can analyse what happened in the last practice and prepare for future practice.
- Perform a post-event role-play. I mentioned earlier that one way of preparing the trainee is to role-play before the trainee performs the task so that they can order their thoughts and prepare. If you could not be present to see what happened then you can arrange for a small, informal role-play following performance so the trainee can explain what happened while it is still fresh in their mind. Do this as soon as possible after the event and use it to assess the trainee's errors and correct performance. Try to provide some objective, positive feedback.

Refining the skills

The final part of the off-the-job instruction process is to arrange for future practice sessions so that mistakes can be overcome and correct performance can be developed.

Summary

In outline, the process for instructing when you cannot intervene as the trainee performs is:

- Teach the basic skills in a safe practice environment where mistakes do not have serious consequences for the trainee.
- Identify a real-life opportunity for practice.
- Before the event, find out if you can be present as the trainee performs. Help the trainee to think through what is to happen by asking questions (see above) and rehearsing or role-playing.
- Before the event, if you can be present as the trainee performs, agree with the trainee what your role will be and how you will explain your presence with the third party. Agree with the trainee what points you will be watching for and how you will review what happens. If you cannot be present as the trainee performs try to establish in advance some method of finding out what the trainee has done and how it was done. For example, if the trainee was required to find out facts from a client, arrange for a report to be written by the trainee and see what factual information is included.
- After the event, whether you were present or not, speak with the trainee immediately and ask questions about their performance. If you could not be present ask the trainee to demonstrate what happened so you can assess its effectiveness or role-play to find out how the trainee went about the task. This is best carried out immediately following the event.
- Use the information you have gained from the debrief to set some training objectives for the next practice event. You will have to gain the trainee's agreement to these as in all probability you will not be present to make sure they are carried out. Try to avoid setting a large number of objectives for the trainee to achieve; it will be too difficult for them to achieve. Instead, make sure that simple skills are developed before complex skills and do not allow the trainee to try and develop and refine more than one skill at a time. Before the next practice event go through the feedforward rehearsal process and agree with the trainee what aspects of the performance will need to be assessed afterwards. Immediately following the event, carry out a debrief as described above.

The instructor's toolkit

The instruction techniques described in this chapter form a toolkit which you can use to develop trainee skill quickly and easily. In the next chapter we will approach effective instruction from this slightly different point of view – the whole of an effective instructor's toolkit will be unpacked and laid out for inspection. This should help you to identify the tools you use now and additional tools you might wish to explore and use in the future.

18

An instructor's toolkit

This chapter provides a brief summary of the range of skills, techniques and activities which are used by effective instructors. The summary has two main uses. First, it shows the range of skills which an effective instructor requires. Second, it provides a framework for assessing your own instructing skills and experience. Think of it as a basic instructional toolkit. Like any basic toolkit it is not complete; you can and should expand it and build on it as necessary.

Effective instructors use a range of techniques to instruct. Like any good craftsperson, they choose and use instructing techniques with care to help achieve particular ends. The techniques which a particular instructor has at his or her fingertips are very like a toolkit from which the appropriate tools (or techniques) are selected, used and returned. The idea of a toolkit of instructing techniques and skills is useful because it carries with it the idea that you must both select the right tool for the job and use it in an appropriate manner.

A toolkit is only as good as the person using it. That person must understand the uses to which a given tool can be put, must be able to select the right tool for the job and must be able to use the tool to achieve the desired result. Some of the tools in a good toolkit have very specific uses and others are useful across a wide range of applications, and so it is with instructional techniques. Some instructing techniques have very specific uses, say for developing particular skills, whereas others have a broader application across a range of skills. The tools in the instructor's basic toolkit described below have a general application.

I am using the term tools in a rather loose fashion to encompass, in some instances, a particular technique (for example, feedback) and in other instances a cluster of techniques (say, task analysis or trainee selection). There is a choice of how to discuss the tools in the toolkit: discuss the tool itself or describe how it should be used. Earlier chapters have described the important instructional tools and so it seems more useful and appropriate to describe the use of the tool – the how rather than the what. For each of the basic instructional techniques there is a description of what the instructor must know, how that understanding can be assessed by what the instructor does and says, and how we can tell from what the instructor does if the technique is used effectively. After all, if instructors cannot explain the use of an instructional technique and cannot show how to use it properly to develop skill they cannot claim to be proficient in its use.

The toolkit – an overview

The instructor's toolkit I describe below contains two main types of tool: tools used for preparing for instruction and tools used during instruction. I cannot really aspire to give you a very comprehensive and detailed toolkit because there are so many ways of going about each of the instructional tasks. Ten different instructors may well use ten different approaches for understanding the task and each of those approaches may be right in that context. So, instead of a fully detailed description of each technique there is a more general description.

If you feel that it is necessary for you to add tools to the toolkit, for example instructional approaches that you use in your particular training circumstances, then it is right to do so. On the other hand it might not be a good idea to delete or ignore toolkit items from those listed below because it really is a basic toolkit and all the items are used regularly by effective instructors. If you fail to use even one of the items listed you run a very real risk of being less effective in your instruction than you could be. In some training circumstances being less than fully effective could have a very expensive aftermath as training times lengthen and trainees fail to perform well!

Here are the contents of a basic instructional toolkit:

1. Techniques to help you understand the skill to be developed:

    - Designing practice exercises and conditions.
    - Preparing the equipment and raw materials.
    - Preparing demonstrations and explanations.

2. Techniques to help you select the right trainee.

    - Preparing the trainee for the training.

3. Investigating and preparing the organization to receive trainees.

Let us look at what each one means in practice.

Tools to help you prepare for instruction

The most important part of being an effective instructor is to instruct as the trainee performs. But you will not be able to do that if you have not prepared well first. So, preparing for instruction is the foundation on which instructing rests. There are a range of techniques which you can use to help you prepare and you will be using techniques that are appropriate for your situation. Rather than describing individual techniques I have described what you will be able to do as a result of using the technique. I have not said how to go about understanding the task by using a particular task analysis approach or package but instead have described what you will be able to do when you have used an adequate task analysis technique. In that way you should be able to measure the effectiveness of whatever approach you use. I have tried to be both brief and comprehensive in my descriptions. Of course that runs the risk that I have been too brief for some and too comprehensive for others. You will have to examine the toolkit and decide what items you should use or discard.

Techniques for understanding the skill to be developed

Chapter 11 pointed out that you had to understand the task from a performance point of view before you begin to help someone else to do the task. Task analysis is made up of a range of activities that depend to a large extent on the nature of the tasks you are helping trainees to develop. Generally speaking, when understanding a task prior to training an effective instructor is able to:

- identify and record (there are a variety of ways of recording what happens – written, film, video, etc. – all of which are useful for later reference and training use) the sequence of operations or actions which are a part of the task;
- identify and record (in some appropriate way) the key points of the task which must be performed in a specific way;
- identify and record the precise methods (procedures or operations for mental or decision tasks, movements and handling methods for movement tasks) which must be used and the points in the task sequence at which they must be used;
- identify and record how to perform the task with due regard for safety and any legal requirements;
- identify and record the task cues that must be attended to or watched for by the trainee, and identify and record how the trainee will recognize them when they occur;
- identify and record how the trainee should react if and when certain events happen (and what not to do if certain events happen);
- identify, design and record efficient organization of work pieces at the workstation ready for task performance;
- identify and record how the trainee should prepare for performing the task;
- identify and record necessary details of equipment preparation, maintenance and storage performed by the trainee;

- identify and record the expected outcomes of the task at key points within the task and at the end of the task;
- identify and record the speed at which key elements of the task must be performed as well as the time in which the task should be performed overall;
- identify and record the quality standards and tolerances which will be used to monitor task performance or which form an integral part of the task's effective performance;
- identify and record how the trainee can tell if things are going wrong and what to do or how to recover if things go wrong.

The aim of the analysis is to help you develop the trainee's skill. Having information recorded (in whatever way is useful and helpful) helps you to make sure that nothing is forgotten and it helps others to use the information and add to it if necessary. Use whatever method works best for you but do not close your mind to alternatives. Similarly, you can identify what you need to know in a range of ways: asking experts, watching others perform the task, reading, watching recordings, etc. Generally, how you go about identifying what is needed is not as important as what you find out. Use whatever method works for you but, again, keep your mind open to possible alternatives.

Designing and using practice exercises

In Chapters 6 and 7 we discussed how skills develop and pointed out that there are different types of skill: open and closed skills, thinking and movement skills. These are organized into a skills hierarchy in all but very simple tasks. Each type of skill needs to be developed in a different way because of its particular nature, and when a range of skills forms a complex task they will have to be developed in a particular sequence for best results. You will need to design practice conditions which are specific to the tasks and skills you are helping the trainees to develop (see Chapter 10). This instructional ability is based on a range of techniques and instructional skills, the details of which will vary depending on the nature of the tasks you are helping the trainee to master. Here is a brief summary of what an effective instructor is able to do when designing practice exercises:

- identify and design exercise and practice sequences that will develop a trainee's physical resources (strength, stamina, etc.) in a manner which is appropriate for the particular trainee and the task they are to perform;
- identify and design exercise and practice sequences which will develop a trainee's mental resources (for example, memory, understanding and perceptual ability) that are necessary for the task to be performed;
- identify and design exercise and practice sequences that will develop the knowledge relating to a task that the trainee must know and understand;
- identify and design exercise and practice sequences which will increase trainee skill in a progressive fashion and which take account of the skills

hierarchy and skill types (open–closed, mental–physical) appropriate to the task;

- monitor the effectiveness of exercise and practice sequences used and re-design as necessary to improve their effectiveness.

The usefulness of a practice exercise is gauged by how well it helps trainees to master the skill. There is always room for other ways of going about developing skill and what works for one person may not work for another. Do not be discouraged. Keep thinking of and trying new ways.

Preparing the equipment and raw materials

If the trainee is struggling with poor equipment skill development will be slow. One instructor was able to double the on-the-job performance of a trainee simply by loosening a screw on a pair of scissors which the trainee had to use to cut thread. If the trainee has to use equipment in the performance of the task you will probably be responsible for their safety until they have the necessary skills, so make sure it is safe equipment as well as functional. In terms of equipment use, an effective instructor will ensure that the trainees are:

- supplied with the right equipment to perform the task at the required standard and that it is in the right condition for use;
- able to operate necessary equipment safely;
- able to start up and shut down equipment safely and appropriately;
- able to clean and care for the equipment they use;
- able to perform basic trouble-shooting and problem identification on their equipment as appropriate;
- able to perform basic maintenance of simple problems or carry out appropriate procedures in the event of a breakdown (for example, what to do, who to tell and what to do until help arrives).

Preparing demonstrations and explanations

I discussed the importance of demonstrations and explanations in Chapters 11 and 12. It is not enough to arrange just any demonstration. The effective instructor will be able to:

- arrange relevant demonstrations which illustrate the task or parts of a task being performed by skilful people;

- as demonstrations proceed, explain to the trainee what the key parts of the task are and help the trainee observe important aspects of the skilled performers' actions.

I also noted that explanations must be performed at a particular stage of skill development if they are to be of most use, and that how you explain has a significant effect on the success of the training. In explanations, effective instructors will be able to:

- explain to the trainee not only what must be done but also how it must be done;
- avoid overloading the trainee with excessive information;
- use the explanation method (visual, verbal, tactile senses) most suited to the trainee and the task;
- attract and maintain the trainee's attention during the explanation by asking questions;
- ask the trainee questions to check understanding or ask the trainee to explain;
- use silence to allow the trainee time to absorb information.

Techniques to help you select the right trainee

Some tasks require the people performing them to have very particular abilities and aptitudes. In some training situations training to required performance must be done quickly. Both these needs suggest that the trainees must be carefully selected, the former by using ability and aptitude tests, the latter perhaps by using trainability tests. In either case the instructor should be able to understand the process of selection and if necessary perform selection so as to avoid unfair discrimination. If selection is important an effective instructor will be able to:

- explain the importance and relevance of trainee selection for the tasks to be trained (to demonstrate understanding);
- explain an appropriate process for choosing appropriate and relevant selection procedures (to demonstrate understanding);
- apply, or arrange to have applied, specific selection procedures in accordance with guidelines laid down by appropriate professional bodies (for example the British Psychological Society).

Preparing the trainee for the training

For the trainee, the training event is a new and possibly stressful experience. Your spending a little time preparing the trainee for what is to come will often help the trainee to perform effectively sooner. It will also make your job easier. So the effective instructor will:

- introduce her or himself;
- explain how they will work with the trainee and what their role in the process will be;
- explain to the trainee what their role in training is to be and what is expected from them;

- explain what help, support and advice they can expect to receive from the training staff;
- explain the training process that is about to occur;
- ask the trainee if they have any questions and explain what to do if they have questions during the training process.

In some training situations it is necessary to prepare the trainee in other ways before the skill training proper can begin. For example, in sport it may be necessary to help the trainee acquire the necessary physical fitness before the sport skill can be developed. The effective instructor in this situation will be able to:

- assess the trainee's physical, sensory and learning resources;
- design training or remedial programmes to help the trainee acquire the necessary resources prior to skills training;
- monitor the trainee's physical and other resources as skills training proceeds and apply remedial measures as needed.

Preparing the organization to receive trainees

I have already pointed out that the purpose of training is to help people do things they cannot currently do. In many industrial and commercial tasks the trainee must transfer from a training function to perform the task at the place of work. It often happens that the way the organization operates is not helpful to the trainee. A similar situation can also arise in sporting contexts; when a new team member joins the new recruit must adapt to the team – but the team can also work to help that process. Whatever the context, industrial, commercial or sporting, an effective instructor thinks about this problem and tries to ensure that the organization is ready to receive the newly skilled trainee in a supportive and positive fashion. An effective instructor will ensure that:

- the trainee is provided with the full range of task skills and knowledge necessary to do the job;
- the trainee is provided with the skills less directly related to performing the task but which are important in working within the workplace (for example, telephone skills or teamworking skills);
- the workplace to which the trainee is transferred is supportive and allows the trainee to apply and practise the skills that have been developed.

Tools to help you instruct

I have briefly explored the tools used by effective instructors to prepare for instruction. I will now describe the techniques used by effective instructors when they instruct. This is the important part of the instructor's toolkit because these are the tools that directly assist the trainee to do rather than just to know. Most of the tools below are activities that take place in a close interplay between you and the trainee. It is difficult to say what is an appropriate level of activity as this depends very much on the trainee, the task and the trainee's rate of progress. I have therefore limited the descriptions to statements about what the effective instructor will be doing rather than how often it will be done.

The tools in the preparation for instruction section were very much optional in that not all of them were appropriate in all instructing circumstances and there were often many ways of achieving the same end point. In contrast, there is much less freedom of choice in this section of the toolkit. An effective instructor will be using all the tools in this section, more or less as they are described. Omitting the use of even one of these techniques will have a serious impact on the trainee's skill development. The following form the core of effective instruction for developing doing skills:

1. Matching what you do to the trainee's stage of skill development.
2. Effective communication during training:

- Matching how you talk to the trainee's stage of skill development.
- Feedforward to avoid errors.
- Feedback styles.
- Correcting errors in performance.
- Measuring trainee progress.

Matching what you do to the trainee's level of skill development

We saw earlier that skills development passes through three distinct stages. I reviewed research that found that effective instructors behaved differently in each of these stages and matched what they did and how they instructed to the stage of skill development of the trainee. That process of skill development sets the context for all the other instructional tools described below. In general terms an effective instructor will:

- be able to explain the three different stages of skill development, what the trainee is learning in each stage and what implications this has for the instructional process;
- provide demonstrations and explanations mostly in the first stage of skill development;
- keep directions and orders to the early stages of skill acquisition so that the trainee has less to remember;
- correct errors immediately in the early stages of skill acquisition so that the trainee is more likely to practise only the correct methods and actions;
- allow the trainee the opportunity to detect and correct errors themselves in

the later stages of skill acquisition to encourage them to think for themselves;

- provide prompts and warnings in the early stages of skill development to help the trainee avoid performance errors and increase the opportunity for them to practise only the correct methods;
- ask more questions in the later stages of skill development and reduce the number of directions and orders in the later stages to encourage the trainee to think for themselves;
- allow substantial opportunity for free practice in the third stage of skill development so that skill becomes fully automatic.

Effective communication during training

We saw in Chapters 14 and 15 that how you communicate with the trainee is of great importance. Poor techniques of communication disrupt skill acquisition and destroy trainee confidence. There are three main areas of communication technique: matching communications to the stage of trainee skill development, feedforward and feedback. I will describe each area in turn.

Matching how you talk to the trainee's stage of development

The effective instructor will be able to:

- be flexible in the methods and style of communication used and will use an approach that is appropriate to the trainee's stage of skill development;
- give the trainee just the information they need, when they need it; give the bare minimum of information needed for the performance of the task at the start of training and, as skill develops, give the trainee additional, supplementary information as needed;
- use silence to give the trainee time to absorb information;
- decrease the amount of talking as the trainee demonstrates increased skill;
- give directions and orders to the trainee as needed in the early stages of training but allow trainees to perform freely and give them time to think for themselves what to do and how to do it before prompting them;
- early in skill development, observe the trainee's performance and warn the trainee as difficult areas present, prompting them to encourage correct performance;
- correct movement errors immediately they occur by telling in the early stages of skill development. In the later stages, correct by asking questions and allowing the trainee opportunity to correct;
- allow trainees to make mistakes (if safe to do so), delay error correction to allow trainee the opportunity to correct the error; if the trainee fails to notice, ask questions to help the trainee think through the error and its correction;
- encourage the trainee to seek information, ask questions and challenge the instructor.

Feedforward to avoid errors

The effective instructor will use feedforward to help the trainee perform using only the correct methods. It is possible to use feedforward as the trainee performs (vital with movement tasks) and prior to performance (important when you cannot be present or intervene as the trainee performs).

Feedforward as the trainee performs The effective instructor will:

- be present as the trainee performs the task;
- be able to explain what feedforward is and its role in skill development;
- understand the task well enough to be able to provide useful and relevant feedforward prompts as the trainee performs;
- be present with trainee as the trainee performs so that feedforward prompts can be provided;
- warn the trainee to attend to visual or auditory cues that are important parts of correct performance;
- warn the trainee to attend to important aspects of the task so that correct performance can occur;
- warn the trainee in good time for them to adjust or prepare their actions accordingly.

Feedforward when you cannot intervene as the trainee performs It is not always possible to be present or intervene as the trainee performs. If that is the case the effective instructor will make sure that the trainee is prepared for the performance by:

- putting aside time prior to the performance to help the trainee prepare;
- asking the trainee questions that will encourage the trainee to think about the task ahead – what they will do and how they will do it;
- exploring aspects of the task which are of particular importance – what is important and how to perform correctly during the important part of the task;
- providing or agreeing with the trainee ways of identifying if performance is going well as the task is performed;
- providing an opportunity for the trainee to rehearse aspects of the task prior to performance and offering guidance and feedback as needed;
- helping the trainee to plan for task performance as necessary.

Feedback styles

If feedforward is concerned with preventing error occurring, feedback has two uses: correcting errors and providing the trainee with information about what parts of the task they are performing well. Both these enable the trainee to perform well in future. In order to give feedback effectively the effective instructor will:

- be able to describe the difference between the four feedback styles (see Chapter 15) and give examples of feedback from each style;
- be able to describe which feedback styles are of most use when instructing (positive–objective and subjective) and explain why they are useful;
- be able to explain that negative–objective feedback is used when the trainee is well skilled and should be followed with an explanation of how the fault in performance will be overcome;
- be present as the trainee performs the task;
- praise correct performance as the trainee performs using objective and subjective styles;
- avoid the use of negative styles of feedback, especially negative–subjective;
- use feedback more in the earlier stages of skill development.

Correcting errors in performance

I pointed out in Chapter 9 that one of the distinguishing features of skill development stage 2 is that the trainee makes many mistakes as they develop their proficiency in the skill. An effective instructor understands that not correcting mistakes immediately will allow the trainee's automatic learning machine to record the errors in performance instead of the correct perform- ance. An effective instructor must:

- be present as the trainee performs the task;
- observe very closely as the trainee performs the task so as to detect errors in performance as they occur or as soon as possible afterwards;
- correct errors in performance immediately in the early stages of skill development;
- allow the trainee to perform freely in the later stages of skill development and give the trainee the opportunity to note and correct their own errors before stepping in to correct them.

Measuring trainee progress

As we have seen, instruction is like a journey – it has a start point (an unskilled trainee) and an end point (a skilled performer) and there is a route between the two. As with any journey it is important from time to time to measure one's progress from the start to the finish to ensure that adequate progress is being made. In instruction, this allows the effective instructor to identify possible problems early and remedy them before they become serious difficulties for the trainee. There is also a second use: you can use the information you gather to encourage the trainee and build confidence. An effective instructor will:

- be able to explain why it is important to measure the trainee's progress;
- be able to describe the most appropriate ways of measuring progress for the trainee's specific training situation;
- use some form of timing to measure the speed at which the trainee is performing if that is an important criterion of task performance;

- use times of individual repetitions of the task as objective feedback for the trainee when building speed on a task;
- use some form of accuracy measure to provide an indication of the trainee's accuracy if that is an important criterion of task performance;
- use records of accuracy as objective feedback for the trainee;
- use measures of performance over longer periods of time (for example, hourly output measures or daily production measures) to measure trainee progress and monitor performance in training;
- use measures of performance over longer periods of time (for example, hourly output measures or daily production measures) to monitor performance after the trainee has transferred from training to on the job.

Using the toolkit

If you can use all the above techniques you are probably a very effective instructor. If you use some of them and not the rest there is probably room for developing your instructional skills. At least you have the opportunity now to sit back and appraise your instructional skill against a model of effectiveness. Do you need to develop further and if so in what directions?

The chances are that if you decide to develop some aspect of your instructional skill further you will look around for training programmes or other sources of information. You can judge their usefulness by comparing the topics covered by the programme with the contents of the toolkit. Many instructor programmes cover knowledge-based instructional techniques – lecturing, dealing with groups and the like – but are they going to develop the areas in which you feel you are weak?

Do not forget that the toolkit outlined above is based on developing the trainee's ability to do rather than to know. It offers you a map of the effective instructor's skills and the techniques they use to develop skill in the trainee.

Index

Building a Better Team
A handbook for managers and facilitators

Peter Moxon

Team leadership and team development are central to the modern manager's ability to "achieve results through other people". Successful team building requires knowledge and skill, and the aim of this handbook is to provide both. Using a unique blend of concepts, practical guidance and exercises, the author explains both the why and the how of team development.

Drawing on his extensive experience as manager and consultant, Peter Moxon describes how groups develop, how trust and openness can be encouraged, and the likely problems overcome. As well as detailed advice on the planning and running of teambuilding programmes the book contains a series of activities, each one including all necessary instructions and support material.

Irrespective of the size or type of organization involved, *Building a Better Team* offers a practical, comprehensive guide to managers, facilitators and team leaders seeking improved performance.

Contents
Introduction • Part I: Teams and Teambuilding • Introduction • Teams and team effectiveness • Teambuilding • Summary • Part II: Designing and Running Teambuilding Programmes • Introduction • Diagnosis • Design and planning • Running the session • Follow-up • Part III: Teambuilding Tools and Techniques • Introduction • Diagnosis exercise • Getting started exercises • Improving team effectiveness exercises • Index.

1993   208 pages   0 566 07424 9

Gower

Coaching and Mentoring

Nigel MacLennan

The coaching/mentoring approach is probably the most effective way of helping others to achieve optimum performance in the workplace. Dr MacLennan's latest book covers the entire subject from basic skills to designing and implementing a tailor-made coaching and mentoring system. He starts by explaining the nature of achievement and the factors that determine it, and then introduces a seven-stage model that will enable managers and supervisors to encourage their people to develop their skills. He examines the problems commonly encountered and shows how to overcome them or, in some cases, turn them to positive account.

The book is interactive throughout, using cartoons, humour, self-assessment questions, case studies and illustrations to reinforce the text. A particularly valuable feature is a set of checklists that together summarize the key elements involved.

Coaching and Mentoring is, quite simply, a comprehensive manual of the best methods known today of helping people to succeed.

Contents

1995   336 pages   0 566 07562 8

Gower

Dealing with Difference

Teresa Williams and Adrian Green

It's the first morning of the training course you've rashly agreed to run. You look round the assembled group and what do you see? Men and women, under-20s and over-60s, white faces, black faces, suits, jeans. Is there anything you can do – anything you should have already done – to make your training effective for people with perhaps widely different ways of regarding the world?

Yes, a great deal, according to Teresa Williams and Adrian Green. In this pioneering book they examine the effects of culture on the learning process and put forward a number of ideas and activities designed to help trainers take account of cultural values in the planning and delivery of their training. After examining both organizational and national cultures they look in detail at how diversity can affect every aspect of the learning event, from the initial announcement, through pre-course work and administration, to running the event itself and the subsequent debriefing and review.

The authors' approach will enable trainers to:
- design learning that acknowledges each participant's culture
- reduce prejudice and stereotyping
- run learning events that do not force participants to compromise their own culture
- achieve a better return on investment by working with the prevailing culture rather than inadvertently opposing it.

Contents

1994   216 pages   0 566 07425 7

Gower

Participative Training Skills

John Rodwell

It is generally accepted that, for developing skills, participative methods are the best. Here at last is a practical guide to maximizing their effectiveness.

Drawing on his extensive experience as a trainer, John Rodwell explores the whole range of participative activities from the trainer's point of view. The first part of his book looks at the principles and the "core skills" involved. It shows how trainee participation corresponds to the processes of adult learning and goes on to describe each specific skill, including the relevant psychological models. The second part devotes a chapter to each method, explaining:

- what it is
- when and why it is used
- how to apply the core skills in relation to the method
- how to deal with potential problems.

A "skills checklist" summarizes the guidelines presented in the chapter. The book ends with a comprehensive matrix showing which method is most suitable for meeting which objectives.

For anyone concerned with skill development *Participative Training Skills* represents an invaluable handbook.

Contents
Acknowledgements • Introduction • Part I Principles • The nature of participative training • Planning and preparation • Briefing • Monitoring • Reviewing • Feedback • Working with people • Part II Methods • Question and answer • Buzz group exercises • Syndicate exercises • Case studies • Demonstration role plays • Skills practice role plays • Projects • Discussions • Game simulations • Fishbowl exercises and behavioural games • Experiential exercises •Support activities • Appendix: Choosing a method • Index.

1994   192 pages   0 566 07444 3

Gower

Running an Effective Training Session

Patrick Forsyth

This down-to-earth guide to planning and delivering a training session will be welcomed by new and experienced trainers alike – as well as by line managers and other professionals with training responsibility. In this book Patrick Forsyth takes the reader step-by-step through the process of structuring the session and preparing materials, before covering the presentational techniques involved in detail. The final section is concerned with following up in terms of evaluation and establishing links to further training. The user-friendly text is supported throughout by examples.

For anyone involved in training, Patrick Forsyth's book represents a painless way to improve performance.

Contents

Introduction • Establishing a basis • Planning the session • Preparing course materials • Running the session: presentational techniques • Running the session: participative techniques • Following up • Appendix: ready-to-use training material • Index

1992   142 pages   0 566 07320 X

Gower

Training Needs Analysis

A Resource for Identifying Training Needs, Selecting Training Strategies, and Developing Training Plans

Sharon Bartram and Brenda Gibson

This unique manual is designed as a practical tool for trainers. It contains 22 instruments and documents for gathering and processing information about training and development issues within your organization. This frees you from the time-consuming business of formulating methods for generating information and allows you to concentrate instead on the all-important task of making contacts and building relationships.

Part I of the manual examines the process of identifying and analysing training needs. It reviews the different types of information the instruments will generate and provides guidance on deciding how training needs can best be met. This part concludes with ideas for presenting training plans and making your findings and proposals acceptable to others.

Part II contains the instruments themselves. They cover organizational development, organizational climate, managing resources and job skills. Each section begins with an introduction which defines the area covered, describes the instruments, and identifies the target groups. It also provides a checklist of the preparations you will need to make. The instruments themselves represent a wide range of methods, including card sorts, questionnaires, profiles and grids.

Effective training requires a serious investment in time and finance. This manual will help you to ensure that the investment your organization makes will achieve the desired results.

1994   176 pages   0 566 07561 X   Hardback   0 566 07437 0   Looseleaf

Gower